Travelling Solo...

... and celebrating life's new opportunities

Jo Cundy

MONARCH
BOOKS

Published by Monarch Books
an imprint of
Lion Hudson IP Ltd
Wilkinson House, Jordan Hill Road, Oxford OX2 8DR, England
Email: monarch@lionhudson.com
www.lionhudson.com/monarch

ISBN 978 0 85721 839 1
e-ISBN 978 0 85721 840 7

First edition 2017

Acknowledgments

Every effort has been made to trace and contact copyright owners for material used in this book. We apologize for any inadvertent omissions or errors.

The text (and extracts therefrom) pp. 15–16 and at chapter openings of "One more step along the world I go" (Sydney Carter 1915–2014) © 1971 Stainer & Bell Ltd, 23 Gruneisen Road, London N3 1DZ, England, www.stainer.co.uk is used by permission. All rights reserved.

Extract p. 35 from Tom Gordon, "Seasons of Grief', taken from *New Journeys Now Begin*, Wild Goose Publications, 2007, www.ionabooks.com. Used with permission.

Extract p. 66 from "Will you come and follow me?", words John L. Bell & Graham Maule, copyright © 1987 WGRG, c/o Iona Community, Glasgow, Scotland. www.wildgoose.scot. Reproduced by permission.

Extract p. 99 taken from Clive Evans, *Time Out of the Ordinary*, used with permission.

Extract p. 108 from "Behold, I make all things new", words John L. Bell, copyright © 1995 WGRG, c/o Iona Community, Glasgow, Scotland. www.wildgoose.scot. Reproduced by permission.

Unless otherwise marked Scripture quotations are from The Revised Standard Version of the Bible copyright © 1946, 1952 and 1971 by the Division of Christian Education of the National Council of Churches in the USA. Used by permission. All Rights Reserved.

Scripture quotation marked ESV is taken from The Holy Bible, English Standard Version® (ESV®) Copyright © 2001 by Crossway, a publishing ministry of Good News Publishers. All rights reserved.

Scripture quotation marked NIV is taken from the *Holy Bible, New International Version*, copyright © 1973, 1978, 1984 International Bible Society. Used by permission of Hodder & Stoughton, a member of the Hodder Headline Group. All rights reserved. 'NIV' is a trademark of International Bible Society. UK trademark number 1448790.

Extracts from The Book of Common Prayer, the rights in which are vested in the Crown, are reproduced by permission of the Crown's patentee, Cambridge University Press.
Common Worship: Services and Prayers for the Church of England (Church House Publishing, 2000) is copyright © The English Language Liturgical Consultation and is reproduced by permission of the publisher.

A catalogue record for this book is available from the British Library

Printed and bound in the UK, September 2017, LH26

"Jo Cundy has, with grace and honesty, shared her 'unexpected journey', travelling solo after the death of her husband. This a courageous book, and I hope that through it many will discover that God gives us the confidence to say 'yes' to opportunities that come our way."

– Rt Revd Libby Lane, Bishop of Stockport

"Jo Cundy writes with easy charm and honesty about the many dimensions of travelling solo. Her book is full of anecdotal wisdom and spiritual good sense."

– Rt Revd John Pritchard, former Bishop of Oxford

"Jo Cundy is the ideal companion for the difficult journey – honest, wise, patient and full of faith. Reflecting her own experience as a solo traveller though the stories of the Bible, she offers insights and encouragement of real depth."

– Revd Professor David Wilkinson, Principal, St Johns College, Durham University

"This is a brave book which gives very helpful insights to those of us who, like its author, have been called, against our will, to 'travel solo'. It is, above all, a journal of Christian hope, an encouragement to 'let go' and 'let God'."

Rt Revd Dr John Inge, Bishop of Worcester

In memory of Susan Kent,
a solo traveller with courage and vision

Contents

Foreword

Most of us who are married or in long term relationships, if we're honest, dread the moment when we will find ourselves on our own again, whether through illness, separation, or bereavement. We know it will come to most of us and we don't know how we will manage. As I watch and am alongside some of those I know who find themselves alone again for whatever reason, I am struck by the fact that one of the greatest challenges is often that of working out how to navigate the tension between the need and desire to look back and hold on to what you had together then, and the imperative to move forward and discover a new life and purpose for the future now.

We got to know Jo and Ian when Ian was Warden of Cranmer Hall – Justin was studying there prior to ordination – and the happy coincidence of their daughter being of similar age to one of our sons and worshipping in the same church meant that we struck up a lasting friendship, which was as surprising as much as it was enjoyable. Leaving Durham at the same time, Justin became a lowly curate, Ian a bishop, but Ian also became one of the mentors and wise godly men who shaped Justin's thinking as he made his way through parish life. Through parties at particular stages in life, time spent on holiday together, and occasional collaborative work we kept up our links and so were aware in part of Ian's last journey through updates from Jo in which she would express far more than the bare facts as she reflected something of the inner journey too.

This journey forward into the unknown is not easy and that is where Jo's lovely book comes in. She balances the anecdotes and stories, which are described with great humour and wonderful illustration, with exploration of the themes round travelling solo in such a way that the resonances of experience will be felt by all, not just those on that solo journey. What emerges is indeed a celebration of life's new opportunities.

With huge honesty and integrity Jo manages to take us back to those pivotal experiences in her own journey and to use them as springboards to discuss some of the issues involved, managing to combine sound wisdom with openness and transparency which draws us in to explore the subject with her. Above all, even as she points us to the joys and challenges of travelling solo, whether now or in the future, she points beyond and around to the ultimate presence, guidance, and sovereignty of Emmanuel, God with us.

Caroline Welby
June 2017

Introduction: An Unexpected Journey...

"And it's from the old I travel to the new..."[1]

... How did I start on this journey?

I close the door behind me, get into the car, and drive out of the Minster Precincts in Peterborough. The removal lorry has already left. I am leaving behind both the place and the memories, and setting out alone, newly widowed, on an unexpected journey in search of a new life – a novice entering the experience of travelling solo.

Seven years later I look back with amazement at where that journey has taken me, and the opportunities that it has offered. Indeed, after nearly forty years of relatively stable life as a clergy wife, I have been discovering the God who does not let the grass grow under my feet and who can provide plenty of challenges in life, and open new doors into the unexpected.

How did I reach this crossroads in my life? How did I come to this point where the road behind is closed and the way ahead is uncertain? How do any of us reach those turning points when life changes completely in ways that may be expected or unexpected, timely or untimely? We come in a variety of ways, gradual or sudden, gentle or traumatic, and we come with a variety of emotions, feeling shocked, bewildered, angry, resigned or relieved. Perhaps we look back and try to trace the route that brought us to this point, and perhaps sometimes we find ourselves asking God why it had to be like this. We each come with our own story, along our own route to a point where we step onto that new path and into a future that is unknown in its potential.

So let me start my story at the beginning. "Once upon a time…" – that is how all the best stories begin. Once upon a time I was a newly retired probate solicitor, married to Ian who was Bishop of Peterborough – with all the diocesan and civic involvements that that job entailed – enjoying a non-executive role in NHS Primary Care, watching our adult children embarking on their lives and professions, and dreaming of eventual retirement to our house in Weardale in County Durham. Then the ordered pattern of life was broken: in the summer of 2007 Ian developed what seemed to start as a chest infection but did not improve; it continued through a wet and miserable summer and an autumn of medical tests, until he was diagnosed with mesothelioma, a rare form of lung cancer affecting the pleural cavity. It was treatable, but not curable, and he was given a limited survival time. An extraordinarily active and eventful eighteen months ensued; a time when we managed to live life to the full and against all the odds, and then Ian died in office in 2009, shortly before we had planned to take early retirement.

It was four months later that I left our tied episcopal accommodation and fulfilled, alone, our retirement plans by moving both to Lanehead at the top of Weardale, where we had a cottage, and also into a little terrace house, an hour away in Durham City, bought to be our geriatric pied-à-terre for when living at 1,400 feet up in the Pennines proved to be impractical. This move into retirement was not working out exactly as I had anticipated, nor as I would have chosen. And it had within it the seeds of a restless life as I moved into two houses in two locations and began to have allegiance to two communities and two different parish churches. I was embarking on a new journey, full of new potential, which might involve all sorts of surprises and challenges.

The language of journeying has always been a popular way to describe aspects of our life from classical mythology onward. Often those journeys are seen to have spiritual significance, to take on aspects of the sacred, to become a pilgrimage. Often in the past pilgrimage focused on the destination, be it Compostela or Canterbury, Rome or the Holy Land, Mecca or the Ganges. In Chaucer's *Canterbury Tales* the journey is seen as incidental, just a time to be whiled away with the telling of stories. Our modern focus has shifted to the journey itself, to what happens en route and what we have learned as we travel – indeed to the point where arrival can almost be seen as an anti-climax. So we need to find a balance between the "why", "where", and "what" questions. Why am I on this road? Where is it going? What am I going to encounter along the way? Like

John Bunyan's pilgrim, we may discern a clear direction, but there may be some surprises along the way.

Some journeys we embark on with enthusiasm and eager expectation. There are other journeys that fill us with apprehension. Sometimes we can decline or divert, and sometimes we do not have any choice. This is a journey that I might not have chosen, but it is one where I have had to face the challenges, put on my metaphorical walking boots, and go looking for the map and compass to guide me along new and unfamiliar paths.

Journeying is a useful metaphor to describe the onward flow of life, and the different phases along the way. Starting a new phase of life is never easy, transitions are not easy, the challenge of the unknown can be daunting. Starting a new phase alone can be even more daunting. It is also tempting to talk about life being a journey as though it were a single continuum, but in reality we know that life is lived at varying paces. There are stop-go phases, the times when we feel that we are going nowhere, the times when we enjoy staying put, and the times when the pace is so great that we just want the world to stop turning.

Each journey is individual and unique, because each relationship that has been lost is individual and unique. We may seek to identify and empathise with fellow travellers, but we can never know the full reality of another person's story – that is for God alone. Likewise, we will all bring to the situation our different material and social circumstances, and our different burdens and bonuses. And it can be good to know that we do not journey alone. The joy and privilege of sharing the journey can bring encouragement, with opportunities for honesty about our successes and failures, and time to laugh as well as cry. We can give confidence to each other to step out on new paths, to explore new places, and to value all our adventures whether big or small.

Our stories may be lived out in a small local context or on the wider scale, in a rural village or a big city, surrounded by family or alone with few relatives, financially secure or struggling, challenged by health and mobility or "fit as a fiddle". We may be old or young, still working or retired. But whatever our circumstances, our stories will have their own unique momentum and potential if we are willing to recognise what is on offer and reach out with courage and faith – one step at a time.

Over the years Sidney Carter's song, "One More Step Along the World I Go", has become a familiar, and perhaps over-used, favourite of many a school assembly, baptism service or wedding, but it has entered into the popular consciousness because it expresses basic truths about life very simply. It is all there – the journey of life, its twists and turns, its joys and sorrows, its hopes and fears. How do you eat an elephant? One bite at a time. How do you journey through life? One step at a time.

> *One more step along the world I go,*
> *one more step along the world I go.*
> *From the old things to the new*
> *keep me travelling along with you.*
>
> > *And it's from the old I travel to the new,*
> > *keep me travelling along with you.*

Round the corners of the world I turn,
more and more about the world I learn.
All the new things that I see,
you'll be looking at along with me.

As I travel through the bad and good,
keep me travelling the way I should.
Where I see no way to go,
You'll be telling me the way, I know.

Give me courage when the world is rough,
keep me loving when the world is tough.
Leap and sing in all I do,
keep me travelling along with you.

You are older than the world can be,
you are younger than the life in me.
Ever old and ever new,
keep me travelling along with you.

[For] it's from the old I travel to the new,
keep me travelling along with you.[2]

As we step out to travel and discover that we are not alone, we meet a variety of fellow travellers coming from different starting points and different circumstances. In Shakespeare's *Twelfth Night* the hapless Malvolio contemplates the random course of life when he says: "Some are born great, some achieve greatness, and some have greatness thrust upon them." Likewise I find myself thinking that some of us are born to single life, some choose to be single, and some have singleness thrust upon them. My starting point as a widow, like that of many other people, belongs in that third group, but I am aware that within that group there are other starting points and other bereavements – rejection, estrangement, divorce, onset of dementia – bereavements which also involve the loss of an intimate relationship but without the finality of death. Solo travellers come in many guises. Each of us has a story to tell and to share, the story of life lived, of ups and downs, of joys and sorrows, of success and failure, and each of us has a future ahead of us to be welcomed and explored.

All these bereavements present challenges as we set out alone. Those who are widowed have to learn to accept the finality of their loss, while for others a partial and perhaps progressive loss means that closure is difficult or impossible. For those facing estrangement or divorce there may be continuing tension and conflict, while those caring for someone with dementia or chronic illness find themselves in a situation where their companion is retreating into a world of their own, a world from which they are shut out. In all these situations there is heartache, and the awareness of being alone. I can share the experience of others who are widowed, and I can try to empathise with the experience of those others whom I have encountered on my travels whose journeys are different but equally challenging.

For each of us challenges and opportunities may come in equal measure. I found that having children scattered not just around England but also overseas, the disrupted retirement plans, the upheaval of moving, the total loss of previous life and lifestyle, and seeking to settle down into not one but two home environments all produced both challenges and opportunities in abundance, and in equal measure. And they brought with them the necessity for travel. With my daughter Liz still living in Peterborough, my elder son Robert living in Leeds with his family, and my other son Paul and his family in Australia, travel was going to be a built-in factor of life. Another element that fed into a restless lifestyle was the legacy of itinerant clergy life resulting in having friends scattered around England and elsewhere. So retirement brings the gift and temptation of "have time, will travel".

However, of course, I have had to realise that travel can become one of the major budgeting issues in retirement! But perhaps in this respect I belong to a generation with certain advantages. I grew up in a post-war climate of frugality and of "waste not, want not", and then married into a clergy life of learning how to make ends meet and yet to keep an open door with generosity. Ian and I could just remember ration cards, enjoyed the wholesome simplicity of the cookery of our childhoods, had been to university when instant coffee and chocolate biscuits were the major indulgence, and started out on clergy life with second-hand furniture and remarkably few of the "essential" gadgets and technologies that now make up modern life. So now, as travel both far and near has become for me one of the major privileges of having time in retirement, it has become also a sobering budget priority, and the bus pass and senior rail card are truly valued.

As we spread our wings, there is a danger that travel can become an end in itself, a way of ticking off the places in the world that we want to see, or the experiences that we want to have. But the bonus for me has been that there have been so many lessons that I have learned along the way and that have helped me to move forward, and so many new doors that have been opened. And the day-to-day journey of homely living has been as instructive as the more adventurous travels – sitting in the armchair in the conservatory gazing down Weardale has taught me as much as any journey by car, train, or aeroplane.

Life is full of surprises and challenges. In the seven years since Ian died I have been travelling a lot of unfamiliar paths in uncharted territory. I have found it curious to discover that, for me, bereavement and retirement have offered so many unexpected opportunities to travel and journey in the literal sense of moving around visiting friends and family at home and abroad, exploring new places, and finding new experiences. When people are being polite they tell me that I am elusive; when they feel less inhibited they complain that I am always away and they never know where to find me or how to contact me. The metaphor and the reality of journeying have mingled, and this book is an attempt to unravel some of those journeys, real and metaphorical, and some of those lessons, as well as to explore this new experience of "travelling solo" in later life, and learn what it has to offer.

It is a book about my journeyings in the world as I have discovered both new places and a new "me". It is about being a solo traveller who has lost her life's companion and who is learning, one step at a time, how to live and journey on alone. It is about finding identity and security and confidence – or about re-finding them. And the basis of each may have changed because we are now "solo" and no longer have an alter ego, a partner who feeds into our deepest needs. And it may take time, a lot of time. What emerges may be different, like a butterfly out of a chrysalis, and may surprise us – indeed might even have surprised our "alter ego". It is about finding new purpose, new opportunities, new directions; a new pattern to life.

Some of us are reluctant solo travellers, but here we are, and we need to get on with finding new paths; we need to equip ourselves afresh, we need to take the first steps. We stand on a threshold and crossing over may not be easy. We may rage against the elements, but eventually the storm will subside, the wind and rain will turn to sunshine, the mists will lift and we may see the longer view more clearly and rejoice in the unexpected beauty of the things we find along the way.

So come with me as I travel from the old to the new, step by step. Come as I embark on a new life and a new identity. Come as I ask some difficult questions, as I share some of the adventures of my travels, as I reflect on things I have learned about how we adjust our lives as solo travellers, as I discover the surprising new opportunities that can open up as well as the pitfalls and heartaches we may encounter, and as I consider how we set our sights to view our continuing future.

Let us venture forth …

1

Venturing Forth Round England

"Keep me travelling the way I should…"

… Am I alone facing the challenges of this journey?

God, I don't want to be alone. Learning to live alone is not easy, and facing the challenge and finding a new way of living, a new way of organising time and activity, is difficult at best and disheartening at worst. Yet, here we are, and we have to get on with it and face each of the challenges and turn them into opportunities. Who will help me face this challenge?

* * *

On any journey we need to have travelling companions. There will be the people we choose to take with us, and the people who choose to join us, and the people whom we meet along the way. Even in a time of loss we know that the network of our friends and family will always play a very important part of our life, and as we embark on solo travel they can become even more important. Our natural instinct in times of trouble is to cocoon ourselves round with the familiar – with people and places and routines that bring the comfort we crave. But gradually we will realise that there is a need for us to go to them rather than expect that they will come to us. For those who have lived very settled lives, friends and family may all be within easy access, but for me as a clergy wife who was on the move for a fair amount of her married life, the problem is that many of those people tend to be scattered across the length and breadth of England. So keeping in contact at a personal level means venturing forth, and inevitably involves a degree of travelling.

I found that such travelling, and being on the move around England, takes time and effort and a serious amount of diary planning, but the blessings that accrue make it all worthwhile. There are shared memories and experiences from the past, and the potential for new discoveries together in the future. And the sharing can work both ways, with support being both received and given. This new phase of life on one's own brings opportunities to empathise and encourage others who are also encountering new challenges.

I think back to the story of Naomi and Ruth in the Old Testament: Naomi, widowed in a foreign country, decides that she needs the love and support of her own family and makes the long journey back home to Bethlehem; Ruth, Naomi's widowed Moabite daughter-in-law, resolves to leave her own country and people and to travel with Naomi. Together they travel, together they grieve, and together they seek a new life with new people in new places. The Bible has an undergirding thread of emphasis on the importance of family, and an awareness that widows and orphans must not be left alone and forgotten but rather be supported. In the New Testament we find this, strikingly, when Jesus, as he is dying on the cross, entrusts his mother to his disciple and friend, John.

Concepts of home, of family and friends, are basic to our stability and our well-being. They give us a sense of belonging and release us from the isolation of "self". Some of us may have lived in the same settled community, town, or village for many years, perhaps even for a lifetime, while others of us may have moved frequently from place to place. When we find ourselves on our own, we find that it is the various networks of belonging that we have created through our lifetime that become a new lifeline to us.

So, as I started to venture forth to visit rather than being visited, I found that the family provided the natural starting point, with daughter Liz in Peterborough, and son Robert and his family in Leeds. The demands of ordinary family life can be comforting in themselves, and I found myself drawn into the familiar roles of "granny on call" or "mother on call". It might be "rent-a-voice for a Taizé service" or "taxi service to a wedding" if I was enjoying the advantages of Liz's house as a B&B within easy reach of London. Or in Leeds it might be babysitting/childminding while the parents have a weekend break, covering when the school has a teacher-training day, or being the convalescence nurse after minor operations. That I have the freedom to do this is a bonus that I value.

Venturing further afield, I have brothers and brothers-in-law who happen to live in invitingly attractive parts of the country, so that Somerset, Norfolk, North Yorkshire, and Oxford have become regular destinations with the potential to use them as a base for other visits. Dodging the snow and ice in Norfolk has become a New Year ritual, and likewise remembering not to choose the week of the Glastonbury Festival for a visit to that area of Somerset. Often the most convenient form of travel has been by car, and en route I have developed an unwelcome familiarity with a range of long-term road works, discovered the limitations of a satnav that doesn't actually have to drive the roads or hills that it/she sends you along, and learned to grade the best and worst motorway service stations.

In addition, many friends remain in parts of the country where we had lived in previous times, and it is enjoyable returning to familiar haunts. Other friends have moved to new and interesting places, so there have been voyages of discovery. These are times to be a tourist and visit new towns, new areas of countryside, stately homes and castles, museums and parks. They are also times to catch up with the way that the lives of others have also moved on and changed. I am blessed with friends and family who have given me excuses to visit Bath, and the Potteries, and Chatsworth, and the South Downs, and Exeter, and Salisbury, and the east coast of Scotland, and a host of other wonderful places.

I am a Londoner born and bred, so I never tire of the temptation to return to the big metropolis, though I am grateful that I do not live there any longer as I try to cope with the immense hustle and bustle that I find now. London offers such variety with its museums and exhibitions, its theatres and shops, its cafes and restaurants, and also its wide range of open parks and the joy of riverside walks. I am immensely grateful for the friends who actually live there and offer me hospitality, and for the ease with which I can reach it by train. Although I learned to drive in London (in the days when a driving lesson could involve going from Hampstead to Marble Arch and back again within the course of an hour), I know that now it is one place where I never wish to venture out in a car again.

While many of the journeys we embark on may have a social purpose, some also will have a more specific purpose, and for those who are still gainfully employed, to a greater or lesser extent, there may be other incentives for travel. We may need to attend meetings, we may be invited to speak or teach, we may attend courses that will extend and improve our skills; we may delve into areas of research, we may want to meet and share with other people engaged in similar fields. For the wholly retired, developing new areas of interest can also give the solo traveller the reason and opportunity to get out and explore new things, to attend courses and conferences, to discover new networks, and to meet new people. For me, venturing to explore the literary world and to write a book opened up the potential to speak about it at meetings and to go on promotional travels. This created the opportunity to engage with a wide range of people, to listen to their stories, and to enter into their world and their needs. In valuable ways all of these things can encourage us to step out and be on the move, and can expand our horizons in every sense.

There can also be some unexpected downsides to venturing out on our travels. Curiously, we may sometimes find that travelling to see family and friends can bring both comfort and challenge in equal measure. I find myself doing familiar journeys on my own instead of as a couple, I find myself seeing familiar people and finding that the relationship has altered in a subtle way because I come now as an individual on my own. This is when I have to have the courage to accept that this traveller is now solo and needs to learn to adjust to a new way of enjoying established relationships, but in the sure hope that these old friendships will continue to blossom and enrich my life in new ways. This is when together we have to find an honest acceptance of what is lost, and an honest welcoming of new potential for the future.

Likewise, we visit familiar places that we have loved and enjoyed together and we may find that the memories they bring back are infused with our sense of loss, our sense of happy times that will not return. It was several years before I could bring myself to go back to the Minster Precincts in Peterborough or attend a service in the cathedral, because I found that my feelings were extraordinarily ambivalent toward those places that had been the context and core of such an important part of my life. There were happy memories, but there was also so much pain around the circumstances of my leaving that I really did not want to return, and indeed my feelings bordered on rejection – the rejection both of and by the places that had mattered so much to both of us.

And sometimes we get caught unawares – I remember, on a visit to my brother in Somerset, going out for lunch at a local pub and realising as we walked into it that the last time we had lunched there we had had Ian with us, when he was clearly very unwell but as yet undiagnosed – and the anguish of living in that painful limbo suddenly came back to me.

At the end of any journey comes the time when we return home, and again we may be surprised by our reactions. Whether we are returning to the familiar home that we shared together, or whether, like me, it is now a new house in a new town, we can find that we have lost the sense that this is where we belong, because some of the essential ingredients that make up a home are missing. It is "my place", not "our place", and it contains only "my things", not "our things". We do not feel that warm glow of "coming home" to an anticipated welcome. I remember returning from my first long trip away from Durham, turning the corner, and feeling a sense of anti-climax. This is home? It took time for me to acquire and to value my own sense of belonging and my own sense of home.

Like Naomi and Ruth, and from necessity rather than choice, I found that I had to start my journeying round England with a major removal to a new home. Clergy life brings the benefit of a variety of vicarages and clergy houses, but they are tied accommodation and with retirement or bereavement comes the need to relocate and start again. Legacies can sometimes be a mixed blessing, and inheriting Ian's retirement plans has proved to be one of them – the source of a degree of inbuilt restlessness in my life. We had always intended to retain both our holiday house at the top of Weardale and our little terrace house in Durham. By the time Ian died we had done work to convert the Weardale house into a more comfortable retirement home and had even moved furniture, books, and other things up there. So for me the simplest thing to do in the limited time available for moving out of the bishop's tied accommodation in The Palace, was to fulfil those plans and move the rest of our furniture and belongings up to the Durham house. Then I had to work out exactly how I was going to find a new base, live in two houses, relate to two communities, and be an active member of two parish churches.

It is not a pattern that I would necessarily recommend, but it has had some interesting results. I certainly do not have the chance to get bored, or feel that I lack occupation or challenge. What has emerged for me is the realisation that the houses offer very different things in their own contexts. The Durham house is in the city and gives me access to College life, to the university, to worship in the cathedral, to lectures, theatre and music, and to easy public transport by train or bus. It is my "activity zone". By contrast, Lanehead is in a small hamlet in Weardale, a mile from the occasional bus, several miles from the nearest shop, and with the different range of local activities that thrive in a rural setting; the view is stunning, and the peace and quiet revives the soul. It is my "creative zone".

My split church life is equally interesting. In Durham I attend a thriving suburban church with people, energy, money, and enthusiasm, even if many folk are stretched and challenged to hold the balance between church life and their day jobs. In Weardale I attend my local parish church which is part of a seven-parish benefice and we struggle with all the problems of rural ministry – too many churches, too few people, and too little money. In both settings we struggle to find churchwardens – in Durham because people are too busy and stretched to take on the demands of a big and thriving church, and in the dale because the congregations are small and there are not enough people with the energy and commitment.

Both environments have been new and have offered the context and backdrop for the task of learning to travel solo. The life that Ian and I envisaged and that might have developed for us together would have been very different from the one that has gradually evolved for me on my own. There is a mixture of the things that have been lost, and of the things that have been gained. The problem of relocation to a new environment is not necessarily a usual problem for the widowed, but affects those who find themselves living in tied accommodation, such as clergy, armed service personnel, and tenant farmers. It may also affect those who have to make a new life in a new place after divorce or separation. The psychologists warn us of the problems of moving at times of such trauma, but sometimes there is no choice.

Although the choice of two locations is a complicating factor, it is one which I have found very creative and liberating in many ways. The house that we bought so that our children could enjoy holidays in open countryside, where they could be free to roam and learn about country life, has become the house where my grandchildren come and escape from urban Leeds to the joys of the Durham dales. They can walk over the fells, build dams in the local stream, discover the joys of snow, visit farming friends at lambing time and learn how to feed orphan lambs and how to accept that the weakest may not survive. On one memorable occasion with three small boys armed with feeding bottles in a pen of orphan lambs, one of them was heard to comment: "There's no point feeding that one, I think it's dead." And so it was.

I confess to an unusual, even bizarre, lifestyle – perhaps another of those things not so much "chosen" as "thrust upon me" by circumstances. One day I will find that "commuting" between two homes will become impractical, and that downsizing to one omni-purpose house is necessary. One day I will find not only that regular drives up and down Weardale are impractical, but that the long distance treks across England become too much of an effort. One day I will find myself taking more regularly to the trains and the buses, and finding new routes and routines for travel. One day even overseas travel may present problems. One day. But for the present this solo traveller will go on making the most of her time and energy, conscious that always, in the end, there is the need to return to a place that is home, that gives stability and a sense of belonging.

Perhaps travel is in my blood – in the 1920s my parents did the long sea trip between New Zealand, where they were born, and England several times, and on one of those trips going back to New Zealand, my mother spent the time stitching an appliqué sampler with the text:

> *Hundreds of stars in the bright blue sky,*
> *Hundreds of bees in the purple clover.*
> *But only one home that I call mine own*
> *Though I wander the wide world over.*[3]

2

Rediscovering "Me"

Step by step "along the world I go..."

... Who am I now?

I have lost half of my identity. I have lost my "alter ego". I am like a bird without a wing. How do I learn to live again, to be me again? Who is this new me? Am I being called not just to do something new, but to be something new? How does this happen?

* * *

My journeying has been not just from place to place, but has involved steps along the way to a new discovery of who I am, of the identity that has been emerging anew as I learn to travel life's path alone. The process is rather like putting a plant into a different part of the garden, into different soil or into a different aspect of shade or sun – or putting a pot plant onto a different windowsill – and then watching the plant thrive in a new way. Anyone who has redesigned their garden will recognise the element of trial and error involved and the sense of satisfaction when the transplant works and the result is literally a "blooming success".

Journeys take time. Any journey of any length takes time, and as we all know to our cost, we are foolish if we underestimate that truism – we will arrive late, miss the train, find the shop shut, be late for the meeting, and have to deal with the consequences.

Whatever the circumstances of loss or bereavement that have brought us to this point of travelling solo, the journey of recovery and rediscovery doesn't happen easily but takes time. Indeed, being realistic, this is one journey that is never actually completed but will always be "work in progress". And it seems that, as with any journey, there are stages along the road. There is plenty of received wisdom from counsellors and psychiatrists indicating the various phases of bereavement, and a degree of objectivity may be helpful, but it may also be helpful to recognise that sometimes "one size does not fit all", and our own journey may be different. I came across and identified with a prose poem entitled "Seasons of Grief" in Tom Gordon's book *New Journeys Now Begin*, which draws on the familiar passage in Ecclesiastes 5 about the times and seasons of our life. It explores the many, often contradictory and emotional, facets that come as we adjust to loss and grief and as we seek to move forward to new life. For me it confirmed the complexity of my emotions and that each journey is individual and may not comply with "received wisdom". In particular the following couplets taken from the poem were helpful as pointers to moving forward.

Every facet of loss has its time…
A time of clarity, and a time of uncertainty…
A time to be thankful, and a time of regret.
A time of giving up, and a time for going on.
A time of living half a life, and a time of wanting to live again.
A time of then, and a time of now…
A time of fruitlessness, and a time of growth.…[4]

Reflecting on my own experience I can identify stages in my personal journey that I went through as I moved from the half life of uncertainty, regret, and the temptation to give up, to times of going on with thankfulness and the promise of growth. The gradual process of moving from "then" to "now" involved first the need for acceptance, then the ability to let go of what was lost, then reaching a point of closure, and finally being released to move on.

As we explore this in greater detail, let me take you to an Ascension Day service in the lovely church at Eastgate in Weardale, where the east window has a stained glass representation of the ascension which makes a wonderful backdrop to a sunrise celebration of the Eucharist on that special day. In our seven-parish rural benefice this was a united service that would be followed by an excellent breakfast in the Village Hall. The preacher on this occasion had spoken of the ascension from the perspective of looking forward to Pentecost, to the coming of the promised Holy Spirit, and waiting to be "clothed with power from on high". But a clergy friend who was staying with me commented afterwards that he saw the importance of the ascension in being a moment of closure for Jesus' incarnational time on earth. This prompted me to do some serious studying of the accounts of the ascension by St Luke both at the end of his Gospel and at the beginning of the book of Acts, and to try and put these into the whole context of the crucifixion and the resurrection.

As I looked at the experience of the disciples through the whole Easter, Ascension, Pentecost story I realised that it embodies an important sequence; it is one that I have thought about deeply as I have looked back at the events in my life, tried to make sense of them, and tried to share my reflections through the media of writing and speaking. The sequence is important and it comprises the following stages:

- Accepting what happens and cannot be changed, and learning an ability to "go with the flow" however difficult that may seem. The disciples had to accept the fact of Jesus' death, with all the horror that entailed, and to accept the failure of all their hopes and expectations. It was a devastating blow, a devastating loss. But the fact that he was dead and buried was inescapable; and as they sought to come to terms with this, to let go of the unique and charismatic teacher, mentor, and friend that they had known, the totally unexpected happened and they were faced with the resurrection. It was a steep learning curve – they were in uncharted territory and could only wait and see what would happen next.

- Learning to let go of what is lost, or needs to be lost. For the disciples life was never going to be the same again. The two disciples on the road to Emmaus needed to let go not only of the physical presence of Jesus, but also of their preconceived ideas about the Messiah. Then as Mary Magdalen encounters Jesus in the garden after the resurrection she is told very firmly not to cling to him; the relationship has changed and she is to let go. We are aware that all bereavement is a process of loss, and letting go of that loss can take time and be a long process. The more dear the thing that we have lost, the more difficult it is to accept its loss, let it go, and move on. As we look at bereavement in its widest sense – not just loss of life with the death of someone close to us, but loss of health, or of possessions, or of dreams and hopes, or of relationships, we know that each can be very painful, each needs healing, each calls for its own process of letting go. And we have to accept that in some cases the letting go will take longer, or may only be partial. I like the following caption to a Leunig cartoon: "God give us strength: strength to hold on, and strength to let go".[5]

- Finding closure. For the disciples after the resurrection there was still the potential to settle into a new set of hopes and expectations for a messianic ministry in Israel, and in Luke's version of the ascension at the beginning of Acts we find them asking Jesus: "Lord, will you at this time restore the kingdom to Israel?"

Their vision was still very limited in its scope, but Jesus' response was to promise a kingdom to the ends of the world, and in Matthew's account of the ascension, to the end of time. The disciples needed the ascension as a moment of closure when their encounters with the resurrected Jesus would be finally gone and his earthly presence with his disciples brought to an end. They had to let go of this physical presence and a geographically limited mission before they could grasp the enormity of what was on offer. Closure, when we find it, is the prelude to the new potential. Realistically, however, there are some situations where closure is not an option and we will have to find ways to balance ongoing relationships and concerns without being locked into the past or burdened by regrets or bitterness. These may happen where we are travelling solo not through the finality of death, but because we have lost our alter ego through divorce or separation, or sometimes where an element of injustice or avoidable error leaves us with an unresolved loss. The long saga of the Hillsborough tragedy is an extreme example that epitomises the trauma of death without closure for so many families who felt locked into the injustices of the past. The challenge to find peace of mind in such ongoing situations is immense but is important.

• Moving on. With the ascension of Jesus came promises for the future. Then and only then could the disciples move on and receive the presence and power of the Holy Spirit among them, a gift that was no longer limited spatially but was everywhere, and this would bring liberating potential. Like the disciples we need to reach a point where we can move on, discover new things, experience liberation and freedom, find new resources. Indeed we need our own Pentecost experience of the Spirit.

• Finding, and enjoying, the adventure of life, and love, and God! Discovering the truth of the African mantra: "God is good, all the time! All the time, God is good!" Learning, as we find so often in the psalms, that hope and happiness are found not by denying the difficulties in life, but by rejoicing that God is alongside to help and guide.

Perhaps some of these stages are incremental and progressive. It does not all happen at once, but can take time – a lot of time. I remember a children's camp in the Quantock Hills in Somerset that Ian and I used to go to, run by a children's evangelist, John Inchley, who used to talk to the children about the ongoing process of "saying yes to Jesus", and pointing out that they would go on "saying yes to Jesus" throughout their lives, making deeper commitments as their understanding grew. In the same way, I think that letting go and moving on can be progressive processes that take time.

Perhaps some stages are more difficult that others, and some situations more difficult than others.

Many painful issues can remain unresolved in our lives, especially where close relationships are involved and our bereavement does not have the finality of death. In Psalm 55 the psalmist expresses the classic longing for flight rather than fight: "O that I had wings like a dove! I would fly away and be at rest." Who has not longed to escape from their troubles like this? But in this psalm of lament there is no easy solution on offer, and perhaps it may help us not to expect early closure, but to echo the psalmist when he ends by saying: "I will trust in God" – whatever!

My own experience of closure came with the publication of the book I had written about my journey with Ian through his illness and the experience of bereavement, *Letting Go of Ian*. As a family we had decided to have the book launch after Evensong in Peterborough Cathedral on the fifth anniversary of Ian's death. It was a great act of courage and of faith, but it was right. We could start with thanksgiving to God for Ian's life and ministry, sharing that thanksgiving in his cathedral church, in the diocese which had meant so much to both of us, and among the people who had loved us and supported us. I could then offer this book as a tribute to Ian and a way of sharing what God had taught us. Afterwards I realised that, for me, this had become a moment of closure, a pivotal point when the focus had shifted forwards instead of backwards. The memories remain and are precious, but I am not bound by them; I have a new freedom to move on.

Other people will find closure in their own way. I have known friends for whom the decision to move house – to downsize, or to be nearer to family – has been the catalyst for finding closure and new horizons. For another widowed friend it was a special occasion at the College which had been a major and formative part of her married life that provided the opportunity to move from "a time of regret" to "a time to be thankful". In the same way that John Wesley distinguished between the dramatic moment of conversion and the later sense of "blessed assurance" in new-found faith, so for us there comes a point where we can move from the drama of loss to the "blessed assurance" of new-found life, and an awareness that, in the words of Julian of Norwich, "All shall be well, and all shall be well, and all manner of thing shall be well."

I find that the ascension is both about closure and about looking forward. Luke tells us at the beginning of Acts that Jesus' final words to his disciples are: "You shall receive power when the Holy Spirit has come upon you, and you shall be my witnesses in Jerusalem and in all Judea and Samaria and to the end of the earth" (Acts 1:8–9). The bereaved disciples were having a crash course in moving on. Here, between the resurrection and the ascension, Jesus is still teaching them and helping them to grasp and understand the wholly new gospel he has brought. With the gift of the empowering reality of the Holy Spirit at Pentecost this will gradually begin to make sense and form the basis of the message that they will proclaim to the world.

I know that moving on, and discovering what God is wanting to do with my life and with me as a person, is an ongoing process. Wherever each of us is on our own journey, and whatever the circumstances that have brought us to this point, we all need to find that momentum and purpose in our lives, and to be enabled to move on. And we all need to find the resources for that journey.

There is a school of management and coaching skills which looks at people as evolving and constantly growing and changing. It seems obvious really, but in the past we have tended to focus on putting people in boxes and labelling their personalities, talents, and abilities. I once found myself at a retreat house alongside a small conference group of people who specialise in "evolutionary coaching", and talking to them I began to think that these principles are of great relevance and use to all of us. For solo travellers it is important not to retreat into a frozen state, trapped by the events that have left us on our own, but to realise that we too are evolving, changing, emerging. We need to grasp these concepts. Think about caterpillars – they come in all shapes and sizes, and may be plain or beautiful, but they too will all grow and change, and one day they will all emerge with a new identity as a butterfly or moth, each with its own characteristics, identity, and role. We may feel that our potential has become trapped in a cocoon of events, but if we can see it as a stage, albeit painful and unwelcome, in our own evolution then we can be released to the discover the new "me".

A nature programme on television revealed that some butterflies migrate and travel immense distances in their short lives. The programme focused on the vast numbers of painted lady butterflies that start out from Morocco in

March and fly north to Europe, even reaching England's green and pleasant land. Many other species of butterfly, however, may remain close to familiar territory. Who knows what sort of butterfly each of us may turn out to be? For me it was becoming clear that, unexpectedly, I might be emerging as a long-distance butterfly, called not just to be someone new, but to be somewhere new.

As we rediscover ourselves, the adventure of finding where we ought to be and what we ought to do is just beginning, and this I find delightfully summed up in an old American Shaker song:

> *'Tis the gift to be simple, 'tis the gift to be free,'*
> *Tis the gift to come down where we ought to be,*
> *And when we find ourselves in the place just right*
> *'Twill be in the valley of love and delight.*
> *When true simplicity is gain'd*
> *To bow and bend we shan't be asham'd.*
> *To turn, turn will be our delight,*
> *Till by turning, turning we come 'round right.* [6]

If we can allow ourselves to "let go, and let God", then we can accept God's gifts and come down where we ought to be. So, come with me as my long distance journeyings begin, and new adventures await as I turn and turn around the world.

3

Australia Beckons!

"Round the corners of the world I turn..."

... How much courage have I got?

How can I find the courage and confidence to step out and do something totally new? And to do it alone? Where do I find the resources of faith, encouragement, and confidence? Who will "hold my hand"? These challenges may be great or small, but they are very real for the solo traveller.

* * *

"If adventures will not befall a young lady in her own village, she must seek them abroad," – so writes Jane Austen in *Northanger Abbey*. If I was not exactly a "young lady" actively seeking adventures, I certainly managed to find them in different ways as my travels further afield unfolded and as I ventured forth to visit my son in Australia and my other relatives in New Zealand. They were not journeys undertaken lightly; they required a lot of forethought and courage before they left the drawing board and the flights were booked and paid for. Perhaps we all need incentives to break out of the mould, and take that first frightening step, on our own, into the unknown. It may not be as dramatic as a trip to the Antipodes, but it may be something that will take us out of our comfort zone, something that offers new experiences in uncharted territory.

Often it is family or friends who offer the unexpected invitation – Would we like to join them on holiday? Would we like to go to the theatre or the cinema? Would we like to join the local community choir? Why don't we take on an allotment? Why don't we take up folk dancing? Or painting? Or karate? Why don't we create the opportunity to visit distant friends or relatives? In the unfamiliar world of being on our own there are still new things to be explored. And likewise there are familiar things that we may have done together with our partner for which we may need help and encouragement to venture forth again on our own.

Perhaps God is good at engineering those inviting incentives for us, and encouraging us to give them serious consideration. Perhaps we need to move from looking inward to looking outward and begin to have an objective awareness of what is going on in our lives and in the world around us, and become sensitive to the nudges from the Almighty. And in my experience, God is capable of both the nudge and the sledgehammer. At some point there will be the potential to embark on something entirely new and we have to take our courage in both hands and say "yes".

It is an encouragement to realise that the Bible is full of examples of people learning to say "yes" to God in unexpected or unlikely circumstances.

Think of Abraham being called to leave a comfortable home in Ur and travel with his family into the unknown, or Moses at the burning bush being told to go back into Egypt with a really difficult and dangerous mission, or Noah being told to build a boat in the desert for a flood that probably seemed unimaginable. Think of Philip sent to join the Ethiopian eunuch in his carriage and explain the Scriptures to this foreign diplomat, or Paul responding to a call to cross the seas and go on a missionary journey into Macedonia with the gospel. And consider Mary accepting Gabriel's outrageously surprising message, and Joseph accepting the potential disgrace of taking Mary as his wife, and then their subsequent journey to Bethlehem, and on to Egypt, which disrupted their chances of starting family life quietly in Galilee. So whether it is the burning bush or the still small voice, the Damascus Road experience of Paul or God quietly telling Ananias to go and restore Paul's sight both literally and spiritually, we need to open our eyes and ears, open our minds and our spirits, and be aware of the potential of what God may be doing.

If that still seems rather daunting, then we need to remember some of the more reassuring verses in the Bible. Isaiah offers wonderful images of God's care for us when he describes God saying; "I have taken you by the hand and kept you" (Isaiah 42:6), and again: "I will not forget you. I have held you in the palm of my hand" (Isaiah 49:15, 16)[7]. These verses helped me through a week at the Taizé Community, on pilgrimage with my daughter shortly after Ian died; a week when God held me and allowed a new place to speak deeply into my grief and to sow seeds of new life. And it is new life that Jesus offers to a hesitant Nathanael at the beginning of John's Gospel when he calls him to join Philip as a disciple, and promises that when he accepts that challenge he will "see greater things than these...[he] will see heaven opened, and the angels of God ascending and descending" (John 1:50, 51). Later, on the night before the crucifixion, when the disciples are filled with uncertainty and fear, he will say: "Let not your hearts be troubled; believe in God, believe also in me" (John 14:1). The Victorians had promise boxes which contained tiny rolled up pieces of paper, each with a Bible promise on it; they were encouraged to take one out at random and read God's promise to them – and there were plenty to choose from. So we need courage to say "yes" to God, say "yes" to the unlikely invitation, and to claim his promises and trust that he will be with us as we venture forth.

For me the unlikely invitation was dramatic as a clear incentive to venture into foreign travel came with the birth of a daughter to my newly married son Paul who was now resident in Melbourne in Australia. If I were to meet this new granddaughter and get a feel for their new life I would have to travel out to see them. It felt daunting, but it was important and necessary. And if I was going to do it at all, then I might as well do it properly, so the time got extended to a lengthy round trip. New Zealand also beckoned, because both my parents had been born and brought up there, and my family history went back into the nineteenth century with early Church Mission Society (CMS) missionaries on my mother's side and émigrés from Northern Ireland on my father's side. It had been some twenty-five years since my only visit with my widowed father, so I planned to go on there from Australia with sufficient time to explore the country, and also to visit a wide range of family and friends. The whole trip, with stopovers in Singapore and Los Angeles, would be a daunting eleven weeks.

A long-haul flight around the world on one's own is not something to be undertaken lightly, and I felt in need of much support and encouragement, so this lengthy trip was planned around friends and family with whom I could stay, who would give me the welcome and the assurance that I needed. Most were people whom I not seen for many years; some were family members whom I had never met before. All had been or were to become a God-given part of my life's tapestry. We do not live in a relational vacuum, and the Bible characters we have considered likewise responded to a call from God where people would form the context of his wider purpose for them as they journeyed on.

It was an exciting trip and I came home with a splendid mixture of memories – of the wonderful range of people whom I met and enjoyed, of mind-blowing scenery and beauty, of exploring new places, of discovering vast tracts of open uninhabited land – be it mountain or desert or rolling grassland, of delving into family history and the pioneer world of nineteenth-century New Zealand, of museums and art galleries, of beaches and swimming, of birds and flowers and trees, of freshly caught and barbecued fish, of spectacular sunsets, and so much more. Looking at basic statistics I reckoned that in the course of those eleven weeks my travel had involved eleven aeroplane flights, eleven coach journeys and six ferry/boat trips; that I had slept in nineteen beds in five countries; and that I had worshipped in ten churches of differing denominations and traditions. I was creating my own travel memories rather than shared memories, but I could still see things through Ian's eyes and wonder how he would have reacted and what he would have enjoyed. It was poignant, but I could still imagine and hope that he rejoiced with me in all that I was seeing and doing. It was a trip that had its high moments and its low moments, times of fun and times of drama, and it was to provide one of the major turning points in my life. It was a "before" and "after" trip.

I especially enjoyed the privilege of being able to worship in a wide variety of churches as I travelled round. There was the packed Anglican church in Singapore where I stopped en route; the wonderful welcome I received at the baptism of my granddaughter in the Roman Catholic church that my son and his family attend in Melbourne; a small but active free church congregation at Bondi beach; a suburban Wellington church; an ultra-charismatic church in Northland, New Zealand; an ecumenical Ash Wednesday service in Auckland; a big, successful Presbyterian church in a suburb of Los Angeles with its numerous congregations, house groups, and Bible studies. These were experiences which broadened my horizons with the mixture of the familiar and the new, absorbing different expressions of faith in different cultures and contexts. Best of all, probably, as a "fresh expression" was "Theology on Tap" – a group who met in a Christchurch pub for theological discussion over a pint and a sausage sandwich.

Part of the incentive and the challenge of the New Zealand part of my trip was to explore the family history as well as meeting members of the far-flung extended family. It gave a specific focus, and allowed me to reflect on the way that families shape our identity and our inheritance. Perhaps subconsciously it was another way of learning afresh to be "me". There is something deep within us that seems to need to search for our roots and discover what has shaped our identity and made us the person that we are. Genealogy can be an all-absorbing hobby for some people, and much depends on your purpose and your priorities in following up lines of enquiry. My brother, in retirement, has become an expert on the naval and military careers of many of our forebears, whereas I am often more interested in where and how people met, what their social circle was like, and how they influenced the world around them. Suffice it to say that I was intrigued by the opportunity in Northland to step back in time and visit the early missionary stations and sites that my great great grandparents, John and Anne Wilson, would have known in the 1830s, to enter their world and to wonder what they would make of my world. And now that I was rediscovering an identity on my own without Ian there was a greater lure to delve into my globe-trotting missionary past and inheritance, to see my life in a wider perspective, both geographical and historical.

There is a rich history here of the brave and committed witness of those first Christians who went to New Zealand with CMS. The mission started in the Bay of Islands and by the time my family arrived was becoming centred round the town of Paihia, which is now a bustling tourist resort on the itinerary of cruise ships – a mixed blessing. Back in the 1830s it was a very small and still quite fragile settlement with a small wooden church, looking across the bay to the more robust whaling town of Kororāreka. Little remains in Paihia of those days, and there is now a stone-built church on the original site, but further north Kerikeri still boasts the oldest original house in New Zealand, a Stone Store, and a wooden church. I could walk the churchyard there and find the gravestone for John Wilson's sister who had travelled out from England to join him when he was widowed to look after him and his four motherless boys, and who had later married and stayed on in New Zealand. These were important links back into my family history, with a sense of continuity not only of the family line, but of the commitment of faith in different generations.

Visiting another mission station at Tauranga where Anne Wilson had died only six years after arriving in New Zealand, I found her gravestone in the mission graveyard nearby which made me reflect on the willingness of that generation to sacrifice so much for the sake of taking the gospel to foreign lands. I live in days of global communication, but before the days of radio, television, and all the instant communications that we now take for granted, it was not easy to know exactly what the reality of your mission field would be. John Wilson had been a lieutenant in the navy, but knew little of what sort of country New Zealand would prove to be. They found the living conditions and the need for so much basic practical manual work challenging, finding that it diverted them from preaching the gospel and planting viable Christian churches.

In Wellington I was able to read original letters in the National Archives and I found one where John, in old age, had described their arrival in a letter to one of his sons:

*One day I climbed up above Paihia and looked across
the Bay of Islands and reflected. What solitude and
desolation I felt as I sat there gazing before me as
to all worldly happenings and prospects. But then
it was for His sake who had endured very different
evils and made infinitely greater sacrifices. It was
sufficient. I felt I was not forsaken.*

It does stop you worrying about yourself when you come face to face with the vision and the challenge, the hope and the disillusion, of other lives. This aspect of my trip was providing not just the opportunity to step out into new worlds, but also the challenge of entering past worlds. And the human problems were much the same.

The reality is that the early missionaries and settlers did feel quite isolated. Although Sydney provided a relatively close point of contact with other Europeans, in the 1830s the journey out from England by sea could take five months and it could take a year to get a reply to a letter home. The last letter written by Anne Wilson to her parents on the island of Jersey was in September 1838, and by the time that they received it the following May, she had died from cancer six months earlier in the November, leaving four small boys aged from nine years to nine months. This was only six years after arrival. She had lived through very difficult times of tribal warfare alongside the problems of setting up new mission stations, but nowhere in her letters or her Journal does she complain about the choice that they had made or lose her sense that this had been God's calling to both of them. Having myself married into a life of Christian ministry, I found here a sobering reflection on the concept of vocation, on our expectations and the reality that unfolds. And here I was, still learning to adjust to the new reality in my life of being left, like John, as a solo traveller. He would survive and adjust and make a new life for himself and the family, and so would I. We have to come to the realisation and the acceptance that God doesn't always do or provide what we expect, and that our commitment can be challenged by his ability to drop the unexpected into our lives.

The unexpected and life-changing experience that would define this trip to New Zealand for me happened on 22 February 2011 in Christchurch Cathedral when a devastating earthquake hit the centre of the city. It was for me a "before" and "after" moment. I had gone into town to visit Bishop Victoria whom Ian had known for many years and whom we had last seen at the 2008 Lambeth Conference. Afterwards I had met a cousin for lunch, but we decided to start with a visit to the cathedral and its shop.

I had bought a book (with a receipt that, in the modern way, recorded the time of the transaction at 12.46 p.m.), and we had entered the cathedral via the north aisle, then decided to light prayer candles in the south aisle. So we were on our knees at 12.51 p.m. when the earthquake struck and part of the tower crashed through into the north aisle. It was a soberingly close call. Whether you call this a nudge or a sledgehammer, it was certainly a wake-up call from God.

I had been indulging in exploring New Zealand's missionary past and my family history; I had been trying to understand the various strands that make it the country that it is today; I had been a traveller and tourist, an observer and learner. Now suddenly I was at the heart of a national tragedy sharing the trauma and grief. Having walked back to my cousin's house in the outer suburbs I was part of the network of bewildered people seeking to support each other. I was seeing New Zealand in a totally different way, and while I was as helpless as everyone else to control what was happening, I was part of a community of people counting their blessings as well as their losses, and getting on with the business of supporting each other and helping to share the necessary practical tasks. Those of us who were thankful to be alive and unhurt could share our sense of gratitude and blessing as we brewed up cups of tea on a camping stove, and shared meals cooked outside on the barbecue. There was lots of heartache as well, as people tried to trace family members who were missing, or heard of houses completed wrecked; the sight of the clouds of dust and smoke rising from the centre of town, and the constant sound of helicopters overhead. Listening to the news on the radio was important but depressing. This was the new world into which I had suddenly been plunged. This was also an entirely new set of emotions that I was experiencing.

Our life can sometimes be described as a rich God-given tapestry, and there are times when we need God-given insight to perceive what sort of pattern he is actually weaving for us. Certainly on that day in Christchurch a whole lot of new strands appeared in my tapestry and a wholly new pattern began to develop. There is a poem that expresses this perfectly and allows us to put the apparently random events of life into a wider perspective:

> *My life is but a weaving*
> *between my Lord and me,*
> *I cannot choose the colours,*
> *he worketh steadily.*
> *Oft times He weaveth sorrow*
> *and I in foolish pride*
> *Forget He sees the upper*
> *and I the underside.*
>
> *Not till the loom is silent*
> *and the shuttles cease to fly*
> *Shall God unroll the canvas*
> *and explain the reason why.*
> *The dark threads are as needful*
> *in the weaver's skilful hand*
> *As the threads of gold and silver*
> *in the pattern He has planned.*[8]

Each of us will have our own unique pattern, and not everyone will find it reworked in quite such a dramatic way. But here I was, dusty and shaken, in a city being rocked by aftershocks and asking God a whole range of basic questions: "What is all this about?" "Why me?" "Why now?" "Why here?" "Why am I not dead?" "What now?" This was not the challenge I had expected when I set out in faith on this round-the-world trip. And I would find that the pattern of the tapestry would continue to unfold as I returned home, and in an unexpected way this event would open up all sorts of new possibilities and opportunities for me. God had chosen the colours, and I needed to have the courage to see what would come next. But that is what living by faith is all about.

4

Opening New Doors

"From the old things to the new..."

... Can the future offer new opportunities?

We are often told that as one door closes another opens, and bereavement does close one door very firmly behind us. The challenge is to recognise that in our new life there will be new opportunities and to have the courage to recognise and open new doors.

* * *

How often have we been told, and how often have we told our children, that travel should open our eyes and minds, and give us new perspectives? We should return home enriched, free and eager to grasp the gift of days ahead of us – a sentiment wonderfully expressed by John O'Donohue in his poem "Blessing for the Traveller".[9] For those of us learning anew to venture forth alone we need to value every "journey", however great or small. The first outing to the shops, or the cinema, or some distant friend, can be as important as a holiday in France or a long-haul flight to the

Antipodes. What matters is making the decision, making the effort, and then enjoying a sense of achievement and widening of our horizons. Each time makes us a little more free to recognise and welcome our "gift of days".

"I looked, and behold, a door standing open in heaven!"[10] When Ian was enthroned as diocesan bishop in Peterborough Cathedral I read this passage from Revelation 4, and Ian preached on the new opportunities that lay before him and the diocese, the open doors, the potential to explore new paths in ministry. In 2011 I was very conscious of the doors that had closed behind me, of what I had left behind after Ian had died and I had moved away from Peterborough to embark on a new life in Durham. I had tentatively opened a new door when I had set out on my trip to Australia and New Zealand, and after the earthquake in Christchurch I was not too certain what that door had really led me into.

About a year after Ian's death and my move to Durham, the Principal at St John's College had asked me if I had changed, and after a little reflection I had told him that I felt that the experience and the upheaval of the last year had indeed changed not only the outward circumstances of my life, but had changed me as a person. When I returned from New Zealand he asked me again if I had changed. This time I knew very clearly that I had had one of those totally life-changing experiences. I had had a near-death experience which had left me asking very profound and basic questions both of myself and of God – Why was I still here? Why did God let me have the continued gift of life?

What was I to do now with my life? What was I meant to learn? My other reaction was to look back over the previous four years and reflect, with some amazement, on just how much God had managed to pack into those years and how an extraordinary story had unfolded. And so was born the feeling that I wanted to write down and share that strong sense of journeying with God through those years and to record all the ups and downs, the good times as well as the bad. I felt that I had a story to tell. A new door was opening – an unexpected door, but an exciting door.

Ah, but the art of writing is not as easy as we may think, and I discovered that there was a lot of hard work involved before I had a text that I was happy with and that a publisher was prepared to look at it seriously. I needed much encouragement and gentle mentoring along the way from the College Principal. I remember showing my first effort to Ruth Etchells, a good friend and a retired English scholar and academic, and being rather disheartened by her comment: "That's a very good start, Jo; now you need to do something with it." But she was right. Sadly she had died before "what I did with it" became a published book, but I think she would have approved of the final published version of *Letting Go of Ian*.

This opportunity to be creative was wonderfully satisfying and therapeutic, and I found that it opened all sorts of doors into new and interesting experiences. Being a novice author can be great fun as I discovered the world of book launches, of interviews, of speaking to various local and church groups. As a lawyer the use of words had been part of my trade, and now I was able to take my gifts as a "word merchant" and use them in a very different way. Both the written and the spoken word could build bridges with other people and with their experiences. And I continue to be humbled by the people who have been able to identify with my story and to find some help and encouragement as they face their own individual journeys through grief and bereavement.

However, there are many other ways of opening new doors in our lives and taking a creative and positive approach to the future. We are all individuals with our own gifts, talents, and interests that God can release and can use. Sometimes the challenges are chosen, and sometimes they are thrust upon us. What is important is first to recognise the potential of what may be on offer, then to have the courage to take the first steps to enter in to whatever is beckoning us, and accept the uncertainty of the consequences. The book *Salmon Fishing in the Yemen* seems an unlikely source of spiritual reflection, but I enjoyed some of its comments on life's journey and mystery, and on what is unknown and unexpected. At one point its main character reflects:

> *I have journeyed this far, to this strange place. The man who started the journey months ago as a staid, respected scientist... is not the same man now standing at a window looking out onto the wild mountains of the Yemen. How much farther will this journey go? Where will it end, and how will it end?*[11]

Ah, if only we knew where and how our journey will end…
but the whole of life is an unfolding of the unknown, so why
not take the risk and go with it? (though perhaps not salmon
fishing in the Yemen). Why not, like Alice in Wonderland,
eat the cake, drink the bottle, open the door, and see what
new opportunities are on offer? Discover talents that we did
not know we had?

The opportunities may include the social, domestic, or
charitable; they may involve new skills, new places, new
groups of people. For me some of the other doors that
began to open up were within my church environment.
Very diffidently I became involved with a regular healing
service in my rural benefice, and found that God was
teaching me to listen to others, to pray for them and with
them, and to develop a ministry of discernment. It was
another humbling experience. And from this grew a desire
to explore the ministry of spiritual accompaniment or
direction. Both of these have been new disciplines for me
and new avenues for walking alongside other people in
the ups and downs of their lives. Both have stretched me
wonderfully, and it is an immense privilege to enter into
the pilgrimage journey of other people and listen to their
stories of seeking to walk by faith.

On a much more mundane level, many of us find that
being on our own, and in my case also retired, we have
more availability and we are in demand to help out with
our families and friends, whether babysitting, monster-
minding, dog walking, looking after the cat, meals on
wheels, or even being a taxi service. Indeed people often

seem to think that we need occupation, that our time should be used and not wasted, and their kindly efforts can be quite demanding, so that finding a new rhythm and balance in life can be difficult.

Sometimes also we need to learn when to say "no". Not every offer, or doorway, or path, will be right for us. I encountered this over the possibility of a new and fairly demanding church role about which I was both tempted and ambivalent. I knew that I needed to hear God's voice – somehow. What ensued was two weeks of fairly intensive prayerful discernment, in the sense that God seemed to bombard me with a sequence of personal encounters with a range of "right" people whose contributions to my thought processes were searching and creative. In the end I had a clear sense of affirmation and of the direction in which God was actually leading me, and I was able with confidence and complete peace of mind to say "no" to the role on offer. It had been an amazing two weeks of journeying with God and listening to him, my spiritual senses had been open and aware, and I had been extraordinarily conscious that every event, every encounter, every element of life, had been able to mediate the voice and hand of God.

As ever, the challenge is whether when we think we hear God's call we are prepared to go out and follow him. Another familiar use of the metaphor of a door in the book of Revelation comes in chapter 3 (verse 20): "Behold, I stand at the door and knock; if any one hears my voice and opens the door...". We are familiar with Holman Hunt's painting of Jesus seeking entry by standing outside a door where there is no handle on the outside, but presumably only on the inside. Here it is clear that the initiative to open the door is with us. And that first "yes" will lead us on to other doors, and other opportunities to say "yes". If we are feeling bruised and battered by the circumstances that have left us on our own, then it is tempting to leave the doors closed. Walking through them into the unknown may be a challenge that we do not want to face. But, as I had discovered, God seems to have ways of enticing us into new opportunities, and of opening up new worlds for us.

John Bell and Graham Maule's hymn "Will you come and follow me?" expresses perfectly both the challenges and the opportunities offered to us by God if we are prepared to look and listen. It highlights that we have the choice to answer "yes" or "no", to accept or reject; the handle is on our side of the door.

Will you come and follow me
if I but call your name?
Will you go where you don't know
and never be the same?
Will you let my love be shown,
will you let my name be known?
Will you let my life be grown
in you and you in me?

Will you leave yourself behind
if I but call your name?

…

Will you let me answer prayer
in you and you in me?[12]

5

Elephants on the Road

"As I travel through the bad and good, keep me travelling the way I should..."

... What are my secret fears?

What are the things buried deep within us that we would rather not face, rather not explore, rather not discuss? We are good at being stoical, at putting a brave face on life's problems, but deep down those problems lurk; these are the fears that do not go away and that we do not talk about. They are the elephants in the room, or for the solo traveller they are the elephants on the road.

* * *

I have vivid memories of coming unexpectedly face to face with an elephant on the Masai Mara in Kenya when Ian and I were having a few days holiday after a visit to our linked diocese in Bungoma. He was a big bull elephant, and the driver of our Land Rover made sure that we beat a very hasty retreat. A few days earlier we had encountered with friends a family of rhinos on the lakeside at Naivasha, and on that occasion it really was too close for comfort; we had to sit tight in our car until all the rhinos decided to move on. We may not all find ourselves literally confronting our elephants, but metaphorically they are still there on the road of our solo journey, so let's try and meet a few.

The most obvious, of course, is the missing traveller, the person who continues to be in our heart and mind, but who is not at our side. Each of us will find a different balance between "hanging on" and "letting go"; each of us will find a different way of moving into the future without losing what is precious in the past. We feel the loss of the person with whom we shared not only our travels but our everyday life, with whom we shared our plans, our hopes, our dreams; the person with whom we could share decisions and laugh or cry when they turned out to be wrong; the person with whom we "did" things. This is true for the wide range of solo travellers, though it may be more complicated for some than for others. If we are separated from our companion rather than bereaved then it may involve a difficult range of emotions as well as practical issues, and the absence is more relative in its nature.

We are missing that significant other. For many this is the person who gave support and encouragement, with whom we shared our hopes and our disappointments, our successes and our failures, the person who gave us security and confidence. Realistically, however, there are those for whom this may also be the person who drained life from us as well as giving life to us, with whom we argued and became angry or weary, bringing a mixture of both comfort and tension. So many threads run through our relationships, but whatever the complicated background the present reality is that we are on our own and we have lost that reference point in our lives.

For better or for worse we now have to find again our own source of security and confidence. We have to find a new belief in our own self-worth, in being "me", in knowing that we are precious to God. Confidence is something that we have to learn again, and it takes both time and courage. It is not easy. Sometimes circumstances help – I would never have travelled round the world alone if Paul had not moved to Australia. On a practical level there may be 101 things that we relied on our "other half" to do, and where we now find ourselves hopelessly adrift. Ian was a DIY man and so I never bothered to learn to wield the screwdriver or hammer, to tinker with car engines, or to regulate the time-keeping and striking of the clocks. So many decisions were made jointly – when the results were good we could share the satisfaction, and when things went wrong we could share the blame together. We have to learn to build on our own strengths and find our hidden talents, and at the same time know when to admit defeat and find help elsewhere.

Even so there may be times when, for whatever reason, life falls apart and we find ourselves facing a major trauma on our own. This is a big elephant – we are without the backup that we have always relied on, without the familiar shoulder to cry on, without the strength and solace that we crave. It may be that we are facing illness, an accident, a family crisis, flooding, or a burglary, or something else outside the run of life's more manageable crises, and the reality is that we find ourselves having to cope on our own.

Where does strength come from in these situations? Are there realistic lifelines that we can hold on to, and realistic ways to cope? Perhaps for starters the following steps may offer a practical way forward. We can:

- nurture the bonds that remain, value what we have got, and the help that is available

- try to create positive potential, try to find a silver lining or a glimmer of light in the darkness

- seek to contain and manage the negatives in the situation

- address the other "elephants in the room" such as anger, despair, the need for forgiveness, the apparent absence of God

- realise and accept that, for the moment, living and loving may be an act of the will rather than an act of the heart.

Not for the first time we may find ourselves asking the questions (as I had done in Christchurch): "Why me?", "Why now?", and perhaps also the questions: "What is this about?", "What do I do now?" I have found that asking "why" tends to look backwards, whereas asking "what" tends to look forwards. So "what" is a more creative question than "why", and tends to lead into "how" which can inject a little bit of momentum into moving forward through our crises.

When life is on its more even keel, there is a "what" question that can still catch us out. It is the more subtle "elephant" in the guise of a friend or new acquaintance who asks: "What do you do?" It is a familiar question, one that is often difficult to answer for many retired people, and even more difficult to answer for someone who finds themselves unexpectedly on their own and not in gainful employment. Couples have often worked out together a general scheme for their lives; they have planned together, set objectives, made decisions. But for someone on their own it seems to require more focus, more determination, and it is easier just to potter along. We realise the extent to which our identity was tied up with that previous life and that lost companion, and there is an emptiness that needs to be filled. But with time, as I have emerged into a new life and done new things, I have found occasions when I have wanted to say: "If only Ian could see me now", or "Do you think that Ian is laughing at us?" Slowly we can become more objective, and we can begin to weave the positive memories into our new life, and embrace our new context and identity. As we become more positive about both "being" and "doing", we can help other people, including our own families, to see that the new reality has both continuity and potential.

When my son Paul decided to get married on what would have been his father's sixty-fifth birthday, less than a year after Ian's death, I was very conscious of a potential elephant. I decided that I was the only person who could address the lurking ambivalence and explain how we had chosen the potential to turn mourning into joy; to have laughter instead of tears. So I was the one who spoke about this at the wedding reception and articulated the emotion that we all felt. And, in a way, Ian became wonderfully present at the celebration.

Another elephant links in to this and is the loneliness that we feel. It is not just the empty house, the empty bed, and the one-person meals; it is the social occasions where we find ourselves surrounded by couples and realise that our familiar partner is an asset that we have lost; it is the realisation that there is no obvious resident companion for theatre trips, visits to exhibitions, or holidays; and it is also the loss of personal intimacy, of someone to hug, to touch, to hold hands with. Whether it is introverts or extroverts who find this easier to deal with is a debatable matter. The introvert is less worried by being on their own, but they may find that they simply retreat even more into their own world, and find excuses not to make the effort to continue to engage with the world outside. Meanwhile the extrovert may be so troubled by the experience of being on their own that they are forced to find ways of breaking out of their isolation.

One solution to solitude and loneliness is to find new relationships, by extending our social circle and making new friends at different levels of intimacy, and this may have the potential to raise all sorts of personal conflicts and dilemmas. How we handle new friendships is highly individual, how we value and remain faithful to the past is highly individual, how our circumstances allow us to move on is highly individual, how we balance past, present, and future is highly individual. And friends and family around us may wish to offer their own advice and opinions, helpfully or unhelpfully. There is no blueprint or easy answer, whether we are bereaved, or are separated by illness or breakdown of relationship. This elephant requires sensitivity, openness, honesty, courage, and discernment. Above all, we need a clear sense that it is God who directs our ways and brings both solace and delight.

Elephants never forget. It is important how we handle ways of remembering and of preserving memories, so that we are not trapped in the past. Our contemporary world has many occasions for "remembrance" – annual services for events such as Armistice Day, Holocaust Day, Battle of Britain, and other past catastrophes, and we are good at creating more of them for occasions such as the centenary events to commemorate critical parts of the First World War. At a more personal level we will remember our own significant dates of loss, churches will hold services on All Souls' Day to remember those who have died, and hospitals may have a "Little Angels" garden to remember babies and children who have died. All of these provide a focus, an occasion, or a place, and these are important for those who are left behind with their memories. We are good at looking back and finding ways of valuing the past, but what our contemporary culture is not good at is finding ways of looking forward with hope and with joy. It is perhaps significant that All Souls' Day is preceded by All Saints' Day, and so sorrow and joy are celebrated together in the context of the Christian hope of resurrection. In France, and other European countries, *Toussaint* is a time when people visit family graves with flowers, and cemeteries can become a riot of colour expressing the beauty of life as well as the sadness of loss. It is good to include the element of celebration so that as we mark significant personal anniversaries we can carry the gift of times past into the present moment and make them special. It is good to have the confidence to celebrate such memories in creative ways, perhaps by having a family day, an outing or a meal, or perhaps alone revisiting special places or walking favourite country paths. We need to have memories that are dynamic, not static. Often on the anniversary of Ian's death I enjoy the open spaces at Lanehead, the place that gave life to both of us, and often one of my children will go cycling and camp out on hill or dale remembering shared holidays and adventures. Sometimes during the autumn half-term we take the opportunity of a week's holiday in France at a place Ian loved, and return with a chrysanthemum to place on Ian's grave for *Toussaint.*

As people of hope, the churches can and should have a ministry in nurturing the bereaved, not just in the initial stages but over the long term, in helping them find new life and new opportunities, in affirming and encouraging, in providing the safe base from which they can step out and travel new paths. We need to help them to build bridges between the past and the future, carrying their memories forward into their new world. We need to help people to find their own sense of vision for that future, and to have the personal courage and confidence to make the positive choices that will help them to move forward. We need to become travelling companions to others and to share our own experiences on the journey. As church communities we need to be creative and imaginative in finding ways of reaching out to friends, neighbours, and colleagues and providing the practical opportunities that open up hope and new life.

And we cannot plead increasing years and old age as a barrier to moving forward. My father-in-law was in his late seventies when my mother-in-law died, and I admired greatly the way in which he quietly and effectively balanced the "gift of days" – indeed the gift of many years – that were left to him on his own. His life remained full: he used his time and talents to support family, to be involved with his church, to run a home Bible study group, and also to learn for himself the domestic arts such as baking and jam-making. Home-made bread, cakes, and biscuits were a feature of tea in his home, and a sticky kitchen floor would indicate the marmalade season.

We need to name our elephants. Indeed as with so many other things in life, we need to name our demons and face them honestly. And for me it is important to name them before God. How do you eat an elephant? One bite at a time. How do you cope with an elephant? One prayer at a time. "God is faithful and will not let us be tested beyond what we are able to bear…"[13] We are back to the basics of faith, to trusting God day by day, week by week, year by year.

I shall not fear the battle
if thou art by my side,
nor wander from the pathway
if thou wilt be my guide.[14]

6

Return to the Antipodes

"More and more about the world I learn..."

... Are there more opportunities on offer?

Solo travelling may offer unexpected freedoms and some "why not?" occasions. As I find new confidence and new patterns, what else may emerge? Will I step out of character and find myself doing new things in new ways? Will I surprise myself?

* * *

Overseas travel can become a habit! The temptation to do Christmas "summer style" in Melbourne with my son Paul and his family was irresistible. Retirement and living solo bring the unfamiliar experience of being able to say "why not?" when unplanned opportunities appear. After years of living with a heavily organised diary – indeed two heavily organised diaries – there is the novelty of being able to respond easily to such an attractive invitation. It does bring the slight frisson of guilt as I wonder if this is just self-indulgence, and it is hard to break the habits of a lifetime

– even harder to make such decisions on my own. But the opportunity to see family and grandchildren in person rather than on Skype makes acceptance definitely worthwhile.

So it was that I set off on another trip across the world, this time joined in part by my daughter Liz. For her, as a primary school teacher, the trip needed to be squeezed into the short two weeks of the Christmas school holiday, but for me it had the potential to be extended both before and after. I was aware of being given another opportunity to explore new things, to listen and learn, to look and see, to interact with people and places. I was also aware that accepting the challenge of the impromptu might just be another way for God to stretch my horizons.

The sun shone and we ate meals outside on the decking, we drank Pimms and barbecued the turkey, we had a Boxing Day walk looking for kangaroos, and, of course, we joined in the traditional church services, but without the carols about snow and deep mid-winter. Most memorable however was to experience Australian "carols by candlelight". Forget the cosy glow of candles in a darkened church, the mufflers and gloves, the smell of wax, the organ and white-robed choir – I was in Australia, it was summer and hot, and they do things differently there. This special Christmas event started at 5.30 p.m. in a Melbourne park as people arrived with rugs and picnics, and the crowd swelled to around 7,000 in front of a large concert platform. We were entertained with a mixture of pantomime, seasonal songs, and the arrival of Santa (to the Australian version of "Jingle Bells", which is hilarious).

Carol sheets and battery-operated candles were handed out – real candles with naked flames were banned. By 8 p.m. the sun was setting and a church choir started to lead the carols with a narrator relating in simple terms the familiar Bible story. And then over the grass behind us came a real donkey led by Joseph and carrying an apparently pregnant Mary and making their way to the front of the platform. As the story unfolded shepherds arrived accompanied by angels (but no sheep), followed by kings with gifts (but no camels). I took my seven-year-old grandson down to the front to see the tableau that was being created, and there at its centre were the young couple, Mary and Joseph, who had arrived with the donkey, now with a beautiful baby (presumably theirs), who was clearly a newborn, only a few weeks old, and smiling contentedly in his manger. We waved our candles – (you can't do that easily with real ones) – and sang "Hark the Herald Angels". Then the narrator moved on to outline the future for this little baby who was born to be the Saviour of the world. In this most secular of countries, the real story of Christmas became an acceptable vehicle for the most amazing public proclamation of the gospel, in the context of the most unusual carols by candlelight service.

After Christmas and New Year, it was on to New Zealand and a chance to return to Christchurch, still fairly devastated and in recovery mode two years after the earthquake. The friends with whom I had stayed were still living as lodgers in a friend's house; the insurance company had still not agreed rebuilding plans for their house, let alone any realistic financial plan. Many unsafe buildings had been demolished in town leaving unexpected wide open spaces, but giving the potential for impromptu art work both in the form of sculptures and of wall paintings. There was a shopping mall made up entirely of converted haulage containers – it is truly amazing what can be done with a few containers opened up and put end to end, beside each other, or one on top of another. The damaged cathedral was cordoned off awaiting decisions about its future, but the transitional "cardboard" cathedral was impressive in its simplicity and its beauty. Designed by a Japanese architect who was used to building for earthquake areas, and made on a triangular framework with enormous cardboard tubes topped with perspex roofing sheets, it is wonderfully light with simple furnishings made of light-coloured wood. It occupies the site of a church that had to be demolished, and is on the other side of the road from the open space previously occupied by the Canterbury TV building where many of the earthquake victims died. On an adjacent site was an art installation made up entirely of a selection of chairs, all painted white – one for each person who died in the earthquake – each chair chosen by friends or family to represent that person, such as a comfy chair for an older person or a child's car seat for a baby. It was a moving tribute and reminder of the personal tragedy that had taken place, a reminder of pain and mortality. I visited Bishop Victoria in her temporary offices next to one of the many damaged churches in her diocese, and heard that she was still living in her two-room "sleep out" hut at the bottom of her garden while the insurers argued over the value of her demolished house. I asked how she coped without a kitchen, and she replied that you could manage fairly well with a kettle and a barbecue. As I talked to people I learned a lot about the capacity for resilience and for creative "make-do-and-mend", but I also learned that the quake itself and its endless aftermath still dominates people's lives and conversation. There is a "before" and "after", and there is a bereavement of all that has been lost from the "before".

Then, just over a year later, the impromptu occasion was on offer again. The son of very close friends was getting married to a New Zealand girl in her home town of Wanganui where my father was born and brought up. My friends needed support – not only was this wedding taking place far from home, but this young couple were already happily settled and working in Melbourne. It seemed likely that, like me, my friends would be need to come to terms with having the newly-weds settling permanently on the other side of the world and perhaps, in the fullness of time, producing grandchildren half a world away. Was this one of God's not-too-subtle nudges? Or was it unashamedly impulsive? And how could I discern where the balance lay and what the right decision should be? The encouragement in terms of "they need you" and "what are the reasons why not?" came from my daughter and from another close friend, and so the diary was juggled, the pennies counted, and the tickets booked.

It became for me another of those "can do" occasions of proving that where there is a will there is a way. Although the wedding was on New Year's Eve, I still managed to celebrate Christmas and Boxing Day at Lanehead with the family before setting off on the long flight to New Zealand, via Dubai and Brisbane, and arriving in time for a "meet and greet" in a local Wanganui pub on the evening before the wedding. This idea of having an informal welcome for guests before the actual wedding was new to me, and I warmed to it. The generous hospitality made those of us in the small overseas English contingent, which only numbered eight including the bridegroom, feel very welcome and at home. A New Year's Eve wedding requires stamina, and we did indeed party and dance until midnight, and then all met up again on New Year's Day for a barbecue in the sunshine.

As I travelled on to visit relatives and friends in other parts of the country, to delve into family papers in the National Archives in Wellington, and then go on to Melbourne to see Paul and the family again, I reflected that this was a good way to start a new year.

This was bonus time. This start was different, unique, and had creative potential. I could forget snow and ice – I had been walking Antipodean beaches. I had been collecting the colourful washed up paua shells on a deserted beach outside Melbourne with my grandchildren. I had joined the early morning dog walkers at Long Bay just north of Auckland. I had run the fine warm black sand through my fingers on the volcanic island of Rangitoto. I had sat on the dunes with a glass of wine on the Kapiti Coast and watched the sun set at one end of the long beach while the full moon rose at the other end of the beach. It was a wonderful bonus to be able to stop and look, to enjoy the beauty and freedom of sea, sand, and sky, and to contemplate the God who knows all the stars in the sky, all the grains of sand on the sea shore, and who probably even counts the snowflakes as they fall.

But I was conscious again that travel is about people as well as places, and I could rejoice in the number of family and friends whom I had seen, in the new people whom I had met, and in the wedding celebration which had been the "catalyst" for the trip. So many stories to share, so much joy and sometimes sorrow, so many hopes and expectations, so much generosity. As I started the new year I wanted to look ahead and thank God for all the people whose paths would cross mine, and to pray for each and every opportunity and relationship that he gives. I might be starting the year in Antipodean style, but when I returned home and the year continued to unfold, it would still retain those opportunities and that potential. I had expanded my horizons in ways that I could take back into my everyday life in Durham, and that could bring new perspectives to enliven the everyday tasks and encounters that make up my home life.

I had rejoiced in the opportunity of the solo traveller to do the impromptu and the unexpected. Along the way I had found new experiences and new insights, and God had indeed broadened my horizons and given me those new perspectives. Realistically, for most of us, such opportunities will not be as dramatic as crossing the world, but are more likely to be more modest occasions, like accepting the sudden offer of a theatre ticket or a trip to an exhibition, the invitation to a meal out, or to go hiking in the countryside, and we need to welcome them. Sometimes this may mean stepping outside of our normal way of life if we are very organised people and being willing to accept a more impromptu approach. But having acquired an unaccustomed freedom it may be good for us sometimes to find the courage to say "yes" to the unexpected and to grasp the opportunities. There are new things out there to be discovered, and the confidence that we need can, and will, gradually grow, and will perhaps even surprise us.

Realistically in a world which is so circumscribed by concepts of "duty" and "right" it is not easy to look at the unexpected offer and say "why not?". We find it difficult to step outside our normal routines, and yet I recall the mantra of one energetic friend of mine who would assert that "we need to take the opportunities of a lifetime in the lifetime of the opportunity." We need to take risks, we need to trust the potential of the unforeseen. Sometimes we need to balance the right use of money, or the environmental impact of what is proposed. We need to accept that we may make mistakes, and that there may be a cost, but we need to see the potential rather than the problems. It may even be that God has a purpose in expanding our horizons. Both of my impromptu trips opened up valuable opportunities to listen and learn, to reflect, and to bring friendship and support into important relationships.

And we do not have to travel the world to find such things. Our impromptu journey can take us no further than accepting the offer of tea with the neighbour next door, or responding to the need for a trip to the supermarket or the hospital to help someone, or going to the cinema with a friend to enjoy a good escape into drama or comedy. Or we may respond to the sort of invitation issued by the Northamptonshire country poet, John Clare:

> *Let us go in the fields, love, and see the green tree;*
> *Let's go in the meadows, and hear the wild bee;*
> *There's plenty of pleasures for you, love, and me*
> *In the mirth and the music of nature.* [15]

These days it is fairly counter-cultural to work in this way, but we may even find that being available for the impromptu becomes a delightful experience that can become a habit, and that the "opportunities of a lifetime" are worth the effort. It is a challenge that is worth accepting.

7

Sharing Travel Stories

"All the new things that I see..."

... How can we share our journey and our story?

We are on a journey of discovery, and we may need to find new ways and new people with whom to share what we are learning and the new things that we are seeing. An important part of our personal journey may be finding ways of articulating it with others. How can this happen?

* * *

"Let me show you my photos and tell you what happened when..." We are all familiar with this scenario, and the long evening that ensues as we look at 1,001 photos of flamingos, or sunsets, or street markets, or whatever else has enthralled our friends who have recently returned from holidays. But it is part of a natural longing to tell stories, to talk about experiences that have mattered to us, unusual encounters, revelations of beauty, or insights into other ways of life that have intrigued or shocked us. We want to remember and we want to share, and we do so through photos, through anecdotes, through the souvenirs and mementos that we bring home, perhaps through food and wine and recipes that we have brought back or remembered and want to repeat.

Likewise, we may want to share what we have learned at a deeper level as we have travelled. There may be insights and revelations that fed into our journey through life, into our faith journey. I am aware that God may have broadened my horizons in a great many ways and the tourist in me may have become also a pilgrim. It has been said that travel may broaden the mind, but pilgrimage refreshes the soul, and perhaps I have enjoyed the benefit of both. What I have missed, however, is the ability to share the memories and the insights with Ian. Without our familiar travel companion, both literally and metaphorically, we have an even greater need to share and process our thoughts and experiences with other people. We have lost our sounding board and need to find another one.

Some people deliberately combine being a tourist and a pilgrim. I remember the thrill of going with Ian on a diocesan pilgrimage to the Holy Land, not just seeing the sights, but praying at the holy sites. On any journey, long or short, far or near, we can be spiritually aware at the same time as we enjoy all that surrounds us and all the activities we are doing. One of our Peterborough clergy used part of a sabbatical break to spend seven weeks walking the long *camino* route of the Via de la Plata from Seville to Compostela. He kept a diary of this pilgrimage, together with a diary of travels in South America during the other part of his sabbatical, and the result became a fascinating book. Reading it I was struck by his reflections on the experience of being a *pelegrino*, walking the *camino*, and living the *camino* life. Asked at one point by a fellow *pelegrino* why he had decided to do the pilgrimage, he reflected on the answer and wrote: "Why am I walking the *camino*? What am I seeking to achieve? What, or who, am I seeking? Is 'getting there' important? Is [walking] important at all?" He concluded with a simple answer: "I am here simply to be; I am not on the camino [just] to walk!"[16] For him the walking had become a vehicle for personal discovery. In a similar way our journeying through everyday life, the new ventures we embark upon, the experience of learning to travel solo through the world, can be the vehicle for us to learn about who we are. In our modern world of compulsive purposeful activity, it is refreshing to reach the point of realisation that, fundamentally, the most important thing is "to be".

When going away on my Antipodean trips my church in Durham has sometimes suggested that I might like to write some brief article for the parish newsletter. So I have had the incentive to stop and reflect more deeply and to weave that into a travel story for sharing. It has been good to link my "tourist" mode to something wider and deeper, to record the beauty and grandeur of the world, the encounters with people, the new experiences, and often the opportunities to share with Christians in other contexts and cultures. My travels have become an integral part of my continuing faith journey, and I have enjoyed the incentive to share the unfolding story with other people.

From time to time the church I go to in Durham has a parish weekend away at the convent in Whitby. A few years ago one of our activities was a craft project in which we took a small square of coloured felt and then used shapes cut from iron-on coloured felts to create on our square a design that would represent our own faith journey. As you can imagine some people warmed to this as a brilliant idea, while some were extremely challenged both in terms of their imagination and their skills. However the results were all wonderfully creative. The squares were then gathered in and put together into a striking banner that now hangs in the church. We were telling our individual stories in a visual way, sharing those stories, and combining them into something new.

At that stage it was only three years after Ian had died, and I was still feeling quite vulnerable as I looked back at the direction that my own faith journey had taken in the previous few years. I had started to put together things that I had been writing in a journal that I had kept during that time, but I felt unable to talk about it publicly or share that story in the various group sessions that we had.

So looking back over my faith journey and trying to find visual images that would reflect that story was quite hard, and it was only after much thought that I finally was able to come up with a simple design. It had three motifs: first the early Christian symbol of the fish which represented my life with Ian from the time we met in a Christian choir called the Ichthyan Singers, and through our many years of marriage and ministry; then a jagged line which combined both the break in my life with Ian's death and also the turning point created by the earthquake in New Zealand; and finally the unfurling coil of the new fern leaf which for the Maori represents the unfolding potential of new life. It had taken a lot of thought and prayer and in the end I was pleased with it and decided that I would take a photograph of it to keep for myself. It had become a vehicle for my faith story and a way of summarising what I saw as key elements in the pattern of my life. Since then I have kept the photo in my prayer diary beside my Bible. It reminds me of God's presence and leading throughout my life and it helps me to pray with thankfulness and expectation as that journey continues; it can be a way of sharing my story with other people in visual as well as verbal ways.

The way in which each of us articulates our faith journey may be very different. If like me you are a "word merchant" then it may be in writing, either privately or for wider publication, or in speaking, be it in quiet conversation, or taking an active part in a church service, leading prayers or giving a talk. But there are other modes of expression that can speak eloquently of our faith; we may use the visual arts of painting or sculpture, or use the wide variety of potential offered by craft work; we may find release in music, in creative use of voice or musical instruments, or in dance and movement. When Ian and I sang in the Ichthyan Singers at university, the choir used to do "musical sermons". In Weardale one of our folk is a brilliant knitter – she knits "prayer bears" to be given to children at their baptism, and she has also knitted an amazing Noah's ark with a full complement of colourful pairs of animals. For the centenary of the start of World War One all the knitters in the dale busied themselves knitting poppies and using this as a way to express something of the loss still felt in rural communities. We can use all sorts of things as vehicles for stories – for bakers special foods can be eloquent, so that, for instance, the traditional simnel cake topped with marzipan balls can be a visual, and edible, reminder of the Easter story – of Jesus and his disciples – and the process of baking your own hot cross buns gives time to reflect and explore the story of Holy Week. Likewise creating and decorating an Advent ring is a way of focusing on our preparations for Christmas and celebrating Christ the "Light of the World" as we light the candles week by week.

More often than not for me, the art of sharing and storytelling is through the written or spoken word. The concept of "the Word" and of God speaking to his people is basic to revelation in the Bible and to our inheritance of faith. The familiar words at the beginning of John's Gospel tell us that "In the beginning was the Word, and the Word was with God, and the Word was God… and without him was not anything made that was made." So in the creation story in Genesis we read that each day: "God said… and it was so." We find God speaking to Moses out of the burning bush, and speaking to Elijah in a "still small voice" as God passes by in his glory. And time and again God speaks in dreams and visions. But God's people are not called just to listen to the word of God, they – and we – are called to share it, "to be ready to give a reason for the hope that is in us",[17] and in the words of the General Thanksgiving in the Book of Common Prayer: "to show forth [God's] praise not only with our lips, but in our lives." We are to articulate our faith, and we are to live it. That is a fairly comprehensive challenge.

Writing can take many forms: it may be expressed in prose, poetry, fiction or drama; it may focus on factual reality, narrative or fantasy; the words may be read silently or spoken or sung. It can be used for celebration or lament, for historical record or declarations of love, to explore philosophy and theology, or scientific research. It is a versatile tool for communicating our thoughts and feelings.

There is a long tradition of people writing about their own spiritual journeys, and employing a variety of literary styles to do so, starting with the *Confessions* of St Augustine, and moving through Bunyan, Dante, Milton, and others. Such "spiritual life writing" spins threads between the sacred and the every day. With the Reformation and rise of evangelicalism the tradition of spiritual autobiography became more popular as a genre developing out of the puritan conversion narrative with its emphasis on rigorous self-examination, individual experience, and personal testimony. It continues to be very appealing to read other people's stories and perhaps to identify with, or be inspired by, their experiences.

Many people find that the simple exercise of keeping a spiritual journal is helpful as a way of listening to their inner self, examining experience, talking to God, and feeling release. It is a place where we can use words in a private context. The journal I started to keep when Ian was first diagnosed with his cancer was a way of articulating the wide range of my thoughts and emotions. It was a place for honest reflection, a place to express pain and sorrow, and a place to chart the stages of a unique journey. Different people will use journal writing in many different ways: some will write daily and some will write only spasmodically; some will just record Bible verses or other ways in which they feel that God has spoken to them; some will write freely with an unmediated stream of consciousness; some will seek to have more ordered material which is reflective and seeking to make sense of their experience; some will analyse the pros and cons of dilemmas which they are facing. A journal can also be multimedia and can include photos, art work, prayers, poems, music, mementos, and any other forms of expression that speak to us. A journal is written now, in the present moment, but we can return to it and use it to reflect on the past and to learn from the past, and there may be things there that we find that we want to share.

My own journal became the basis for the writing of a book. I needed to draw on its random entries and take them into the realm of literature, I needed to make a serious attempt to edit it and create something coherent that would tell the story of the faith journey I had walked alongside Ian, and afterwards on my own. I was trying to spin the threads between the sacred and the everyday in a way that would speak to other people and would encourage them on their journey. For me, this creativity finds expression through narrative, but other people may craft their writing into poetry, or fiction, or drama, and spin similar threads thereby.

Whether we feel called to use and share our talents as a writer or an artist, as a musician or a craftsperson, then this may be a calling and a gifting that raises a lot of profound questions. As a writer I ask myself whether I am being called to articulate my everyday experience of faith in the context of the upheavals of the twenty-first century? Is this tradition of spiritual writing a way of discovering the gifts that accompany our griefs? Am I called to express an acceptance of the place where God has put me, however unwelcome and unexpected? Am I called to seek the sacred within the blemished beauty of a messy and complicated world, to search for glimpses of beauty beyond the blemishes, and to find ways of expressing and sharing this? Those who feel called to express themselves through other artistic mediums will need to ask similar questions. Any form of testimony demands honesty as we look at ourselves and at the world around us; and any form of testimony is searching for the sacred, for the revelation of God at work in our world and in our lives.

A Visiting Fellow at St John's College in Durham gave a seminar for Christian writers which drew attendance from an interesting range of creative students and young writers, and raised all sorts of basic questions such as: Why do we write? Whom do we write for? Where is God in our writing? Why do we publish? For me this focused my thoughts to ask the question: Do we, do I, have a sense of God's purpose and God's calling? And I realised that I had published because I had a deep, even driven, desire to share what I had experienced and learned. I had received the call of God to use the gift of words, and a new and unexpected vocation had opened up for me in my later years. So the challenge for all of us is to discover what individual gifts God is calling us to use, perhaps in new and different ways, and to run the risk of becoming equally driven to use those gifts to share faith.

Our churches are places where we should nurture the gifts that the members of our congregations have for sharing their faith and telling their stories. They should be places where we learn that we can express our faith and our worship in a wide variety of ways – in music, in poetry, in art, in dance, and where we can share our experiences whether of everyday life, or of the more adventurous things. They should be places where we use this variety of our gifts and talents to explore new ways of reaching out into our communities, sharing and engaging them in discovering the journey of life and the journey of faith. We have a "good news" story to tell. Our young people go away on gap years and return with new insights and stories to share. I went to New Zealand and returned with a story not just of travel but of God's protection and guidance.

As I have travelled, both literally and spiritually, I have learned the importance of sharing our journeys and our experiences – both the joys and the sorrows – of telling our story, of encouraging one another, empathising with one another. We all have a story to tell, and it will have highlights and lowlights, it will have valleys and mountain tops, it will have bits we may want to forget and suppress, it will have times of achievement and of failure, it will have "God moments" that surprise and delight us. Our story will have the potential to help other travellers on life's road. When did you last have a "God moment" and tell someone about it?

8

Valuing the Present Moment

"Ever old and ever new..."

> *... Am I living in the past, the present, or the future?*

I want to hang on to all the memories and the good things of the past, and the future can be a frightening unknown. So how do I cope with living in the present moment?

* * *

The writer of the fourteenth-century *Cloud of Unknowing* says: "God, the master of time, never gives the future. He gives only the present, moment by moment."

There is a danger for those of us who are travelling solo that we can often feel that our present is a limbo in which we are caught between our past story and our future hopes. But the exciting potential is there for us to wake up and embrace the present moment with enthusiasm. Each moment is still precious, and we will not pass this way again. Indeed, time seems to get more precious as we get older and the realisation impresses itself upon our consciousness that it is finite.

The office of morning prayer in Common Worship has a prayer that echoes this sense of anticipation for the potential of each new day: "The night is past, the day lies open before us, let us pray with one heart and mind. As we rejoice in the gift of this new day O God, set our hearts on fire with love for you now and always." And the psalmist says: "This is the day which the Lord has made; let us rejoice and be glad in it." Our moments and our days are pure gift from God, and how we use them is our choice.

In a recent BBC *Thought for the Day* on Radio 4, Sam Wells, Vicar of St Martin in the Fields in London, spoke of his dilemma when watching the Tour de France pass through the place where he was on holiday in France – whether to watch the cyclists as they raced past in the twinkling of an eye, or to record the moment with a photo. I remember exactly the same choice a few years ago at Chaumont on the Loire, but on that occasion the peloton were pedalling uphill and there was time for both.

He commented that in our desire to preserve the present moment, we so often choose to build a bank of records that we may never access again, rather than to trust our memories to cherish and retain those valued impressions. Instead there are times when we need to learn to value the present moment, refrain from the desire to record, retain or embellish our lives, and just live them – now. Our photo albums, journals, and diaries, however valuable, can sometimes be a distraction from living.

As we become aware of the present moment we may become more attuned to the world around us; we may learn to listen and to see in new ways, and find ourselves encountering the God who speaks and acts. How often have I, have you, been in church and felt that a particular reading, or hymn, or prayer was meant directly for you? How often has a random decision led to an important encounter or conversation or event? How often have you been stopped in your tracks and said "Wow, God, that was meant to be!" We need to become truly aware of the world around us, of the importance of opening our eyes to see and opening our ears to hear. Jesus told many parables to encourage his hearers to see the world in a different way. One of those was about a merchant who bought and sold pearls, and how one day he found the perfect pearl, a pearl of great price, and so he sold everything he had in order to buy it. The image here is of discovery and revelation, and it comes in the context that Jesus gives as his preface to the parable: "The kingdom of God is like…" We are invited to contemplate not just that eternal treasure might exist, but the ways in which we might find it. Jesus gives a twist to what his hearers might have expected to be a standard rags-to-riches story – the point is in the finding and what the finder does to make sure of his treasure. They and we are asked to see the kingdom both as a treasured thing and as a process, as something not just static but dynamic.

In his poem "The Bright Field", R. S. Thomas draws on this parable of the merchant finding a pearl of great price, and explores how the seeking and the finding are linked and are both valuable. He describes perfectly our temptation to hurry on, or to hanker back, and in so doing to lose the glimpse of glory, the shaft of light, that has illuminated the field. And as the poem values the fleeting delight in the finding of the hidden treasure of the pearl, so it encourages our delight in the present moment so that we can stand, content, between our past and our future.[18]

We all live life at different paces – some of us are naturally active and busy, outgoing, disciplined and organised; some of us prefer a quieter and more withdrawn lifestyle; some of us combine a bit of both. But for all of us there is the need from time to time to stop, to reflect, to slow the pace of life and take note of the world around us. "What is this life if full of care we have no time to stand and stare?"[19] Many of us need to get away from the guilty feeling that our time should be "filled". There is a wonderful passage in Edith Wharton's socially perceptive novel *The Age of Innocence* where the central character is staying with his in-laws, a family who lived by the principle that people's days and hours should be "provided for", and in response to an enquiry from his mother-in-law as to how he proposes to spend his time that day he replies paradoxically: "Oh, I think for a change I'll just save it instead of spending it."

Different spiritualities and different traditions give us insights into ways in which we can "stop and stare", and take stock of our individual present moments. There may be hidden depths to our limbo that may hold surprising promise. We all have different temperaments and are at different stages on our journey, so some approaches will resonate with us more helpfully than others.

Ignatian spirituality encourages the practice of "Examen", a simple exercise at the end of the day whereby we take time to make a regular review of what that day has held, to consider what we are grateful for and what we are not grateful for, to consider what brought life into our day and what drained life out of it, what made us happy and what made us sad. There is a healthy honesty about this, whether it is done privately or in a small and intimate group. It allows us to acknowledge God at work in our daily lives and to assess our response, to be realistic about both success and failure. There will be times when it allows us to express our anger and disappointment, as well as other times when we want to rejoice and give thanks. For me it seems that it fits naturally alongside the evening liturgy of Compline, that late night service which was once described to me as a "dressing gown and slippers" service. Examen as a daily practice allows us to savour our time and acknowledge God's gift of days; it allow us both to give thanks for the good things in the day, and to experience regret for the things that could have been done better. What has God given today? Where have we perhaps glimpsed a pearl of great price?

The Orthodox tradition is more contemplative with a focus on self-awareness and identity. In the saying of the "Jesus Prayer" there is a search for inner stillness, for being open and available to God, and for finding an awareness of me in the here and now. This is a way of valuing not just the present moment, but the present me. Our identity matters, and the prayer brings us and our needs to Jesus. "Lord Jesus

Christ, Son of God, have mercy on me, a sinner." It allows us to be realistic. It allows us to rely on Christ's mercy as we move forward. The following prayer comes from a Benedictine house, but echoes the same theme:

> *Be silent, still, aware,*
> *for there in your own heart*
> *the Spirit is at prayer.*
> *Listen and learn,*
> *open and find,*
> *heart wisdom,*
> *Christ.*[20]

This use of silence and stilling of the mind is also found in the practice of mindfulness, which comes from an eastern tradition but has much to offer to our Christian understanding. It teaches that being more aware of the present moment can help us to enjoy the world around us, and understand ourselves better. It encourages us to become conscious of our thoughts, and of the sensations, sights, sounds, and smells all around us. And it encourages us to stop regretting the past or worrying about the future, and to nurture a positive attitude with a focus on community and interdependence. For some this allows them to connect in a positive way with the richness of life around them, while for others it may seem a rather cerebral approach.

By contrast there is the newly popular Danish concept of "hygge" (pronounced "hooga"). This is something which may appeal not only in the dark depths of northern winters, but also in the dark depths which lurk and surprise us as solo travellers. It is said that with nine books published in one year on this theme that it is the greatest export from Denmark since Lego. This is a philosophy that encourages enjoyment of simple pleasures allowing us to accept and live more fully in the present reality and context. So, we could start by finding a candle, a flower, a warm rug or a book – whatever it is that gives you, or me, comfort and joy in this present moment; something that reinforces us not just physically and emotionally, but spiritually. And we can enjoy time with friends, with a glass of wine, or a cup of tea; time spent in giving and receiving; and time spent taking the opportunity to bring beauty into the darkness. It is, for us, a reminder of the beauty, the love, and the peace that Christ brings into the world by his incarnation. It combines being kind to ourselves with being kind to others, and sharing a more gentle and simple way of life that allows us to live more fully.

As we seek to live more fully and contentedly in the here and now, we may also find that we want to revisit the balance between living in the present moment and valuing our memories. There is indeed a place for those memories, for recording what we see and what we hear; for recording those precious moments and pearls of great price. How we do this and provide our own aide-mémoire will be very individual. When Ian became a diocesan bishop I was aware of a whole new lifestyle opening up involving events and contacts which spread beyond the church and into the life of the city, the county, and the country. On arrival Ian had received a rather splendid five-year diary from English Nature who had offices in Peterborough and, deciding that I could find a better use for it than he could, he passed it on to me. I started to record, very briefly on a daily basis, the immense variety of things that made up the life of a diocesan bishop and his wife. It was all so new and mind-blowing; I recorded the highlights and the lowlights, the struggles and the rewards; I recorded the wide range of people and places who became part of our life and part of this ministry of leadership. Thus started for me a daily habit of reflection.

Then when Ian was diagnosed with terminal cancer I started to keep my journal as a private place where I could be completely honest about pain and sorrow, surprise and disappointment, insights and reflections, unexpected blessings; a place where things both profound and mundane could all be poured out. It provided release and comfort. It was a way of talking to God when conventional prayer eluded me, and it was a way of recording those "God moments" when I was aware that he had spoken or acted.

Many things may help us to retain the memories – words, photos, music, clothes, furniture, ornaments – all the many things that have associations or recall events. But they need to become part of our present life now; we cannot dwell in the past like Miss Havisham in Dickens' *Great Expectations*, and perhaps we need to find new ways in which they can be shared and enjoyed in some way. One of my greatest joys was seeing Justin Welby wearing Ian's cope and mitre for his enthronement in Canterbury Cathedral and realising how proud and delighted Ian would have been.

By whatever route we have found ourselves unexpectedly travelling solo, we find ourselves standing on a threshold where there is a "before" and an "after". As our circumstances have changed, so inevitably we have changed, and we cannot return into the past. We can perhaps learn from the incident recorded in Mark's Gospel 8:26 where Jesus cures a blind man and then instructs him not to go back into the village. Why? Because having crossed the threshold into vision, he would have to adjust his life; it would no longer be lived in the world of blindness, but new vision would mean new pastures, and learning to have a new relationship with his village. As we adjust and embrace the opportunities that may be offered by the new life that is opening up, we may perhaps set ourselves some challenges. One of my friends decided that as she reached the age of seventy years, she would try and do seventy new things in the year ahead. However ambitious or modest, it is always good to set ourselves targets.

Accepting the "new" in the "now", learning to be "me" in the present moment, may be a challenge, but it may be part of what God wants to open up for us. We have to find the balance between "being" and "doing", as God calls us not just to *do* something new, but to *be* someone new.

John Bell's simple chant comes to mind inviting us to recognise and grasp what Christ is offering in the here and now:

Behold, behold, I make all things new,
Beginning with you and starting today.
Behold, behold, I make all things new,
My promise is true, for I am Christ the way.[21]

9

Letting God Speak

*"Where I see no way to go, you'll be telling me the way,
I know..."*

> *... How do I hear God speaking to me?*

We know that we need the reassurance that God is there as we travel on, and in the words of a familiar hymn, I know that I need to hear him "speaking in accents clear and still", and I need him to "speak and make me listen".[22] But do we have the eyes to see and the ears to hear? Are we open to those God moments of revelation?

* * *

Travellers collect all sorts of tales and experiences which have enlivened their journey – tales to tell around the fire on winter evenings, to amuse or encourage. Jesus did so much of his teaching in parables, by starting with the ordinary things in life and telling stories that would be open up new meaning. He opened people's eyes so that they saw things in a different way. And perhaps we should not be surprised that the ordinary things of life can speak to us sometimes. So come with me as I share a few revelatory moments that have come to me along the way as I have travelled, both literally and metaphorically – enjoy a little bit of serendipity. They are stories that are linked by the way that they explore the patience and trust that we need to have as we journey on and explore the new things that we find that God is doing in our lives, the new doors that he is opening.

They are, if you like, the random milestones or markers along the way.

The unwelcome mole… (when things go wrong…)
In my rural Weardale retreat at Lanehead, I finally got round to sorting out a bit of the garden that had been the essential vegetable patch for the working family who originally lived in the house in the nineteenth century. I decided I could manage to keep about a third of it as a flower border and then I had turf laid on the rest. A year later the grass was beginning to look really quite good and established, and then… overnight I found that my lovely lawn was covered with little "runs" and with tunnels going down into the earth beneath. A mole had been at work and had, unusually, decided to have fun running over the surface rather than digging around underneath and sending up the usual piles of earth. I was gutted. All my hard work, all my satisfaction at having done a good job, all my hope for the future of this bit of garden – and a "little gentleman in a black velvet waistcoat" had laid waste to it all! But on sober reflection I realised that there is a niggling grain of reality in this situation – life is so often like this. We think that we have

begun to recover from the past, and to lay new foundations for our life, and we are full of optimism, and then suddenly something happens that blows us off course. And like my mole, it may be something quite small and insignificant, but the effects seem huge in our perception. My mole catcher tells me that the lawn will recover in time and indeed as the grass grows the runs and tunnels are less visible. Likewise with us, eventually those unexpected, unwelcome, and untimely setbacks in our lives will heal over, and we will find ourselves back on track. Mind you, it may not be quite the same track, because God may have used the experience to guide our feet into something new.

This makes me aware of those who, as they struggle to come to terms with a bereavement, find themselves unexpectedly having to cope with a family crisis, or with serious illness, or with some other loss or unwelcome situation. The question is always "why?", because we feel that coping with one problem at a time is enough. Perhaps we are more vulnerable at such times and we struggle to find the faith to hang on and keep a sense of perspective. I well remember the sequence of crises in the week after I moved from Peterborough to Durham, as my new car was broken into, my new larder cupboard fell off the wall, and I succumbed to a bad attack of food poisoning. It felt like time to say to God; "I've had enough!" But this was reality and I had to get on with damage limitation and keep going.

It is another of those times when we need the gift of acceptance of what has happened and need to find the faith and trust be able to say with Julian of Norwich that "All shall be well, and all shall be well, and all manner of thing shall be well". The lawn will recover.

Theology of the scraps… (feeling abandoned…)

It was a bold, potentially foolish, decision to go with my daughter on a pilgrimage to Taizé just four months after Ian had died. But I desperately needed a break from all the continual activity at The Palace and I needed some space and time for myself in a different context. It had the potential to be halfway between a holiday and a retreat.

I was moving from a low point where the future felt empty, where I was just a lost and lonely soul constantly on the verge of tears, and moving to a point of acceptance that I might actually be precious in God's sight. The Bible studies in Mark's Gospel were revelatory as we looked at the two accounts of the feeding of the 5,000, and the feeding of the 4,000, and wondered why Jesus told the disciples to gather up the fragments that remained. As we linked this to the encounter of Jesus with the Syrophoenician woman, it became clear that every crumb and every picnic fragment had its own importance – the scraps mattered to Jesus. So let us consider this more deeply.

The frugal housewife knows the importance of leftovers, and how to use them creatively – think of Christmas and all those recipes for brilliant new dishes and "réchauffé" using up the turkey, the ham, the cold sprouts, and potatoes. How much more might God know the creative value of the person who feels left behind, left over as one chapter in life closes? He is the God who says:

- "I have called you by name, you are mine" (Isaiah 43:1)

- "You are precious in my eyes" (Isaiah 43:4)

- "The birds of the air... Are you not of more value than they?" (Matthew 6:26).

He is the God who gathers the scrap because it is precious, who gathers us up because we are precious in his sight.

The Bible has many significant instances of rejection leading to a new and different future.

Think of Hagar – the slave woman rejected and cast out – losing her status in Abraham's household as Sarah's maid and the mother of his firstborn son. She is given a promise for a different future as God meets her in her despair in the desert and speaks to her.

Think of God's care for Israel as they lost their status in Egypt after the death of Joseph, and his provision of a new future for them in a "promised land".

Think of God's care for the remnant of Israel after losing their homeland and being exiled to Babylon, and then their rehabilitation in Jerusalem under the heroic efforts of Nehemiah.

My Taizé experience taught me several important lessons: that God meets us and speaks to us through the Bible (basic really, but important to hold on to); that he provides release and space when we need it; that he provides support, perhaps in unexpected ways – I had the support of the group from Durham with whom I had travelled, the hospitality of the Brothers, and the prayers of faithful friends at home. These were perhaps obvious lessons, but they were timely and much needed. And Taizé also taught me the importance of looking for future times when the opportunity may arise to step aside, find this sort of reviving input, and recharge the spiritual batteries.

We who are left after any sort of bereavement are either consciously or sub-consciously aware of that status of being left over from our previous context. There is a loss that diminishes our sense of self-worth and of purpose. We can get stuck in an emotional limbo, unable to go back, and not wanting to go forward. But once we recognize the amazing intrinsic value of the "left-over scrap", then with conscious effort and courage we can decide to pick ourselves up, dust ourselves down, and start all over again. Indeed, whenever we find ourselves in a situation where we feel alone and bereft there is the consolation of knowing that we are neither isolated from, nor forgotten by, the God who cares for us as he also cares about every little sparrow (Matthew 10) and every lily of the field (Matthew 6).

Escape from a botanic garden… (laughing at the unexpected…)
It was a lovely summer afternoon in Auckland and I went with a cousin to a delightful botanic garden which climbed up the hillside, crowded with flowers in full summer bloom, and gave splendid views over the city to the sea. We took our leisurely walk, regretted the closed cafe, and arrived at the exit gates… to find that they were closed and padlocked! We had failed to take proper note of the opening hours, and there had been no friendly warning bell or staff member

walking round to alert us. Instead, here we were, facing two very fine eight-foot wrought iron gates with elegant spikes on top, in a quiet cul-de-sac with nobody in sight. We contemplated, and indeed attempted, various ways of negotiating gates, fences, and hedges, and I was quite proud of my ability to reach the top of the gates only to realise how very effective spikes are in deterring one from crossing over to the other side. Finally a woman at a neighbouring house who was putting out her rubbish bin came to our rescue by supplying both welcome bottles of water and the phone number of the security firm responsible for the gardens. Two hours later we were released and were on our way home to panic over arrangements for the dinner party planned for the evening. As we had pondered the prospect of spending a night among the roses, it had taken a little time for us to see the funny side of the experience. Perhaps we should be more thankful to God for the gift of humour and laughter, and cultivate our sense of what is funny, peculiar, or ridiculous.

I remember my mother telling me that the three most important things to nurture were humour, humility, and humanity. Not a bad blueprint for life. And not a bad blueprint for those of us travelling alone in life. There will indeed be times to laugh, and times to cry, and we need to recognise and value both. If we come to situations with the humility to admit that we may not have all the answers, and the humanity to see things through the eyes of other people around us, then we will be sensitive to the balance between sunshine and sorrow, laughter and tears, the serious and the light-hearted. Humour can be a powerful medicine and, rightly used, can heal a lot of hurts. We are often told that it takes more muscles in our face to frown than to smile, (some claim that the ratio is 43 to 17), so it makes healthy sense to see our life from the bright side, and to help others to do likewise.

Gift of the fern leaf... (celebrating creative gifts...)
My trips to New Zealand have offered to me another image which I have found helpful. It is the Maori motif that they call "koru", based on the unfolding and unfurling of the fern leaf on the forest floor in the bush as the new growth appears each spring. It symbolises new beginnings, new life, and speaks to them of peace and harmony and tranquillity. I had written about this at the end of *Letting Go of Ian*, looking back at the unfolding story of my own life over those eventful years. A year after its publication I had a surprise parcel from the friend in Los Angeles with whom I had stayed during my first world trip way back in 2011. She is one of those people who is wonderfully creative with fabric, needle, and thread, and she designs and makes beautiful quilts both for practical use and for hanging on display. She had read my book, and then when shopping had unexpectedly found the perfect background fabric with an overall base repetition of a motif exactly like the koru design. So she had taken this as the basic fabric on which to create an amazing design for a wall hanging. This parcel was her gift to me of the fruits of her creative labours, and it was stunning. The timing of its arrival was also stunning.

It was at the end of two weeks of intensive prayer trying to resolve difficult options and to discern what God really wanted me to be doing with my life, time, and talents, and here was a gift that was affirming in visual form the gentle and continuing unfolding of his plan for me. I felt humbled by the gift and by its timing, and I wept tears of gratitude and of emotions too deep to name.

Often we carry with us, perhaps subconsciously, an abiding sense of loss, and yet there are times when we can be overwhelmed by sudden and unexpected generosity. This gift was so special, a wonderful token of love and friendship expressed in the use of amazing creativity and talent. There will be times when we are the recipients of such lovely gifts, and then times when we also will be able to give to others tokens of our love and gratitude, and use whatever talents and gifts God has given to us so as to bring pleasure to someone else. This may be in little ways like the gift of flowers, or a homemade cake, but it is the two-way process of giving and receiving that brings joy into our lives. There are many different ways of giving, and we can also give of ourselves and what matters to us. We may pass on something of the past into a new future. For me, seeing Archbishop Justin Welby wearing Ian's cope and mitre for his enthronement in Canterbury gave me immense pleasure and a sense of continuity into the future. Perhaps, as we travel, the joy of gifts and of giving may be like the finding of fresh-sprung fern leaves along the side of the path that we are walking.

Growing mustard seeds… (small beginnings…)

"The mustard seed… is the smallest of all seeds, but when it has grown it is the greatest of shrubs and becomes a tree"[23] – while botanists argue over the accuracy of this image, it does make for an excellent and dramatic parable. At his service of installation, or enthronement, our current diocesan bishop in Durham chose this passage from Matthew's Gospel as the theme for his sermon, exploring this parable that Jesus told where he uses the mustard seed as a metaphor for the kingdom of God. A bookmark was distributed with a picture of a tree with a bullet-point summary as a prayer reminder that this simple parable could be the vision for growing the gospel and growing the people of God in the diocese. The day of this service was in fact 22 February 2014. On that same day in New Zealand they were marking the third anniversary after the earthquake in Christchurch, and at the same time in Hamilton they were consecrating and installing as bishop of Waikato the daughter of Durham friends of mine, who had been ordained in the Church of England and gone to New Zealand some three years earlier. So many different strands were linked and coming together on that day. For both Durham and Waikato there was a new bishop, a new ministry, and the opportunity for new growth. In Christchurch there was the ongoing, and still painfully slow, emergence of new life after the earthquake. And in my mind all this linked with the general concept of what grows from small beginnings, and gradually becomes mature and useful.

In so many ways we need to believe in the "God of small beginnings" who can grow great things from our small seeds of faith and our tentative steps forward. We may not feel very confident as we take those solo steps into the future; we may, like the people of Christchurch, feel battered by what has happened to us in the past to set us on this path. But if we can nurture that small seed of faith, it can grow and flourish, little by little. The fern leaf may become a beautiful frond; the mustard seed according to the parable becomes a useful tree or bush. We need to rejoice in God's ability to take our small beginnings and enable us to blossom into something beautiful and useful. Who knows what surprises might be in store, and what sort of tree we will become?

The bonsai gift… (struggle for new life…)
When I left Peterborough the Dean and Chapter gave me a very splendid two-feet-tall ten-year-old bonsai ginseng. I felt that this was one of the more challenging leaving gifts that I received, and the bonsai and I have had our ups and downs ever since. After a year it had withered, lost all its leaves, and feeling a mixture of despair and guilt I had put it into a corner of the garden for the summer before finally consigning it to compost. But miraculously it started to re-grow and produce new shoots and new leaves. And now? Well, the bonsai is not the perfect shape that it once was; it is more luxuriant and untidy, somewhat shorter since it refused to regenerate along the full length of its ample trunk, but it has a continuing life. And here am I,

still thriving but with a life that is less disciplined and more random and adventurous that it used to be – I too have wilted and revived and found that life does not regenerate in exactly the same old way.

The layby… (taking time out…)
I thought, as a car driver, that I knew what a layby was, until I went to Australia for Christmas. There the big stores offer "LayBy" so that you can choose your special Christmas present six months ahead and then they will "lay it by" while you buy it by instalments until just before Christmas when you go and collect it. The ultimate disaster happened to my daughter-in-law when we arrived in Christmas week to collect the dolls' house she had chosen for my granddaughter: the store couldn't find it in the LayBy room, and they had sold out. Meltdown ensued, all round. But there was a happy ending because we were offered a choice of bigger and better dolls' houses at no extra cost (save that of finding extra room for it at home).

Laybys – those little oases for escape beside a busy road, sometimes bypassed bits of old road still tree-lined and secluded, more often litter strewn run-offs where the traffic still thunders by. In France they rejoice in the name of "aires de repos", which are often attractive sites for a picnic.

Generally we resort to a layby when we need to stop, take a break, revive our flagging spirits, find new energy. Sometimes it is because we are lost and need to find directions, or other problems have arisen. We all need that "welcome break" when we are travelling – be it the big bustling service station, or the quieter layby.

So it is with our travelling through life. We need times to step aside and stop, times when we can be clutter free, travel free, with no timetables to keep, no responsibilities. They can be times when we can focus on books, or music, or craft work, or walking, or whatever feeds our inner being. Most of all they can offer time to think, to reflect, to plan, to check our life directions.

The wartime slogan "Keep Calm and Carry On" has taken off in recent years and spawned a multitude of variations. But it is a mantra worth playing with and considering as we stop in our layby. What is the encouragement that we need at this moment? Keep calm and…? What? Keep calm and… travel? explore? discover? Keep calm and… reflect? pray? listen? learn? The psalmist encourages us to "Be still and know that I am God", and it is in moments of calm that we find deep knowledge, and recognise our deep desires.

A little bit of serendipity…?

I wonder how you hear God speaking to you? It is just as well that we are all different and experience the world in our own way. It means that as we share our own unique stories, and our own perspectives, we can enrich each other's lives. I have shared some of the ways that I have seen God at work in my life and the lives of people around me; the ways that I have found encouragement and direction on my journey. George Herbert, in one of his poems entitled "Prayer (I)", excels in his metaphors and descriptions of the ways in which he encounters God:

> *Softness, and peace, and joy, and love, and bliss,*
> *Exalted manna, gladness of the best,*
> *Heaven in ordinary, man well drest,*
> *The milky way, the bird of Paradise,*
> *Church-bells beyond the stars heard, the soul's blood,*
> *The land of spices; something understood.*

I wonder in what ways your eyes and ears are opened and your senses attuned to see beyond the mundane to the divine, to see "heaven in ordinary", to encounter God in the everyday, to find "something understood"? I wonder what unexpected blessings you find?

10

Blessings Abound

"Leap and sing in all I do..."

> *... Do we really allow ourselves to rejoice and count our blessings?*

D o you ever stop and say to yourself: "I am so lucky"? Do you reflect with thanksgiving? From my house in Weardale I can stretch my eyes and look down the dale over a pattern of fields and walls, trees and sheep, the evening sunlight casting a golden glow (and perhaps highlighting the less welcome molehills). One day my journeys up here will become impractical, one day I may have to relinquish this beauty, but just at present I think how lucky I am and I thank God for the beauty and peace.

* * *

The Lord bless you and keep you;
the Lord make his face to shine on you and be gracious to you;
the Lord turn his face toward you and give you peace.

Numbers 6:24–26

This Aaronic blessing is so wonderfully comforting and affirmative. We want to be held, to feel at peace with the world and with ourselves, to feel that there is sunshine on our path. It is what we want for ourselves, for our family, and for our friends. We pray it for those who are setting out on a new path in life; we pray it for those who are encountering some kind of trouble; we pray it in trust and expectation. Like so many other wonderful Bible texts it has been set to music, and as I write the sound of John Rutter's anthem is running through my head.

So what does it mean to be blessed? Is it the same as being happy? We are told that our English word "happiness" has as its root the word "hap", which means chance. But the implication here, as in the Beatitudes in Jesus' Sermon on the Mount, is of a blessed state that is serene, that touches us deeply, and that is independent of the changes and chances of our fleeting world. Jesus talks of a joy that endures when he tells the disciples, on the eve of his Passion: "I will see you again and your hearts will rejoice, and no one will take your joy from you" (John 16:22). This is the paradox and mystery of faith, that in the midst of pain we can experience God's blessing.

How can we manage to see beauty through our pain, through what is broken and ugly and lost? Sometimes our pain and grief seem to have an all-embracing scope – touching us, our family and friends, our community and country, the world and its nations, and the groaning of all creation. How do we see beauty and find blessing? Perhaps only by making a conscious effort to find positives, to be creative, to value every little glimpse of light through the cracks in life, to recognise every fleeting presence of the Spirit. And it is in this way that we may find the hope that leads to faith, and that brings us back to the experience of God's blessing.

Sometimes we may feel abandoned, as the disciples did, and wonder if we will again feel joy and want to praise God. I remember back in the 1970s the rather glib use in some church circles of the irritating acronyms PTL and PTLA – "Praise The Lord" being the response for times when things went well, and "Praise the Lord Anyway" being the response for times when things went badly. It seemed a rather superficial approach to the way we viewed the ups and downs of life, but as so often there was a deeper nugget of truth because it sought to acknowledge God's presence even at times of failure when we felt abandoned. It was a reminder that faith sometimes has to be an act of the will rather than of the heart.

What does it mean to be blessed? So often in the last few years there have been times when, as I have stopped and reflected, my reaction has been to feel immensely blessed. Somehow, despite all that has happened, despite the trauma of walking a road through terminal illness, bereavement, and relocation, there has been the awareness that the Lord has indeed kept me and blessed me.

When I went for a week to Taizé just four months after Ian died I realised, subconsciously, what a number of my praying friends realised very consciously: that this could be a risky exercise. But I found myself claiming God's promise in Isaiah: "I have taken you by the hand and kept you..." I sought and found God's gift of healing and of peace. It is at such times that we discover the many layers that there are to God's blessing; we discover how to come to terms with the past, the present, and the future; we learn to discern some pattern in the apparent tangle of our lives.

Should we pro-actively seek blessing? There are good precedents in the Bible. In Genesis 32 Jacob wrestles with God until daybreak and will not let him go unless God blesses him. In 1 Chronicles 4, in the midst of tediously long lists of genealogy we come across the brief enigmatic reference to Jabez calling on the God of Israel and saying "Oh, that you would bless me". So why do we hold back?

Is it a natural reticence and politeness, a hangover from childhood, that tells us that we shouldn't be asking for things for ourselves? Yet God invites us to come to him, to seek his face. Psalm 14:2: "The Lord looks down from heaven upon the children of men, to see if there are any that act wisely, that seek after God." And in Luke 18:41 Jesus addresses the blind man who cries out to him on the road to Jericho with the words: "What do you want me to do for you?"

What do we ask for? Jabez had a clear idea of what he wanted from God – he starts with a simple request: "Oh, that you would bless me". And Jabez is clear about the shape and content of the blessing that he requires and needs:

- to enlarge his borders

- to have the hand of God on his life

- to be kept from harm and pain.

So what would we mean by similar requests to these? Some may be obvious, but as we travel solo what blessing would be appropriate to our life and our needs? For example, might our "borders" be interpreted to mean the sphere of our activity, our involvements, our ministry? Do we hope that as God guides us with his hand and protects us from harm he will also lead us on into new areas of life? We need clarity and honesty in what we are asking God for. For those of us who are travelling with unfinished business, can we ask for blessing on those people and situations that are unresolved? The simple and open-ended request for blessing can be a means of bringing healing both to us and to other people around us. And we have a God who takes the initiative – in Psalm 18:16 "[God] reached down from on high, he took me, he drew me out of many waters." He is a God who finds us in our need, and can both pick up our lives and open up our lives.

The psalms have a lot to offer to us as we search for ways of understanding blessing in the context of our complex lives. In his *Companion to the Evening Psalms* the former Dean of Durham, Michael Sadgrove, comments that in the psalmist's relationship to God nothing is held back. "This is 'prayer without pretending'; for every experience whether of light or shade, of exaltation or despair, of bitterness, resignation or trust is laid bare before the God to whom 'all hearts are open' as the Prayer Book collect puts it."[24] He also comments that for the psalmist being "happy" or being "blessed" is having "a right assessment of human life and, in particular, discerning where God is to be found in it."[25] Hence one of the enduring and endearing aspects of the psalms is that the whole of human life seems to be laid bare before us with its whole range of emotions, and we are encouraged to engage with it openly and honestly.

One of the privileges of living in a cathedral city like Durham is the opportunity to join in the daily offices of Morning and Evening Prayer and to pray the whole psalter regularly each month according to the disciplined ordering in the Book of Common Prayer. Blessings and prayers that have been used by people of faith for centuries, even millennia, continue to be the liturgical means to express worship, confession, and intercession in today's world. I find that one of the benefits of having belonged to choirs and done a lot of singing over the years is also that so much of the psalter can be sung and has been memorably set to music; in this form it has entered deep into my subconscious with the ability to surface again with delight at all sorts of random moments. I think of the deceptive simplicity of Taizé chants, the majestic settings in oratorios, the gentle flow of plainsong and Anglican chant, the metrical psalms and hymn versions, the polyphonic anthems that soar heavenwards.

What does it mean to bless? And who may do it? "Bless you" – it slips off the tongue so easily as a form of endearment, as a response to a kind action, as the sympathetic comment when someone sneezes (and even, in irritating common parlance, without the pronoun!). If being blessed is about having a sense of wholeness and fulfilment, then is the act of blessing about our desire to pass on this expectation of the riches of God's grace? We who have discovered and know that the Lord is gracious want others to have this experience, and want to be the source of blessing to others. This goes beyond our prayers of petition and into areas of praise and promise.

One of the aspects of getting older is that our friends and contemporaries are doing likewise. The aches and pains and physical irritations of anno domini that we try to ignore are beginning to afflict them in equal measure! There can be lots of laughs as we compare notes, but at the same time we want to walk alongside them, provide support and encouragement, and remember them before God with thanksgiving and with prayer. And as the years progress there are more deaths and bereavements – some of which seem far too premature. I have a prayer list of "we who are left", filled with lots of lovely people for whom I grieve, and with whom I empathise, but whom I also hold before God for his abundant blessing as they, like me, journey forth alone on a new voyage of exploration. At the beginning of my small prayer diary I have two words with which I try to keep a creative balance as I bring people, situations, and events before God – "problems" and "opportunities" – because most things contain the potential for both. There is a similar balance in the words of a familiar hymn: "bane and blessing, pain and pleasure, by the cross are sanctified". It is a challenge to realise that our role may be to become a means of blessing to others, to our families, friends, and communities. But in God's world, no experience is wasted. It is worth noting how often a psalm may start in anguish as a lament and yet end with praise.

It is humbling in today's world where there is so much need and pain, to realise that I am blessed with health and strength, with material comfort, with family and friends. But it is encouraging to see this in context and to realise that God's gifts are given to be used. Blessings are about enjoying the favour of God in tangible form – but with the purpose of honouring God and his will for our lives. Blessings are to be shared; it can be a two-way process and the giving of blessing can be as life-giving as the receiving. It is worth reflecting when reading the Sermon on the Mount that Jesus gives two parts to each beatitude and that there is give and take built into the structure of this teaching on blessing. So, "blessed are you who are peacemakers, for you shall be called children of God", and "blessed are you who mourn, for you shall be comforted"; "blessed are you who are merciful, for you shall receive mercy."

If we feel blessed, then we need to go out into our communities and share that blessing. It would do our doom-laden pessimistic world a lot of good if it could hear the voice of thanksgiving and blessing. Isaiah says, "I will turn their mourning into joy and make them rejoice from their sorrow." We can be those who have learned that God does indeed bring comfort to those who grieve, and is indeed able to turn our mourning into joy, and so we can reach out to others to share that sense of blessing. We can challenge those around us to rejoice and to count their blessings.

Bless the Lord, O my soul, and forget not all his benefits.

Psalm 103:2

11

When Travelling Days Are Done

"Give me courage when the world is rough..."
                ... How do we befriend our own mortality?

L et's face it, immortality is not an option – the aches
     and pains of ageing come to us all, and so eventually
     will death. How do we prepare to face this and to
"befriend" our own mortality? As a solo traveller this can be
a sobering challenge. It is another lurking "elephant".

* * *

Shakespeare was not far off the mark in *As You Like It* when
Jacques, in declaring that all the world is a stage and we
men and women are only players, describes our seventh
and last age as being: "Sans teeth, sans eyes, sans taste, sans
everything" (even if he did forget the ears!). Alas, how true
that, as we age, those vital senses that keep us in touch with
the world around us, with its people and its pleasures, begin
to diminish. Ageing is another of those truths that have to
be universally acknowledged.

   As solo travellers we have learned about letting go and

leaving things behind, about losing a familiar travelling companion, and we have embraced the many opportunities of our new road and learned to welcome and enjoy all that our new life has to offer. But realistically we will get older, we may have accidents, mishaps, random illnesses, and bits of us will begin to function less well. And, yes, immortality is not an option, and the daunting prospect of facing it rather more on our own than we might wish, is one of those rather bigger "elephants". We have been used to having someone with whom to share the really deep things in life, our hopes and our fears; we have been used to having someone with whom to walk the darkest paths. Now we need to find other trusted travelling companions with whom we can be similarly open and honest. This may be a friend, a family member, an ordained or lay member of a church, a spiritual director, or someone else in whom we feel we can confide. And indeed, as we become attuned to the need, we may also find that we ourselves are drawn into this sort of sharing role for someone else on a similar journey.

So perhaps we should give some thought to how we face our future, and perhaps the following pointers could start us off as the basis of an "action plan".

- We need to make the most of our time, our health, and our strength. Whatever our talents and our circumstances, there is a whole world out there to enjoy, a life to be lived, work to be done, experience to be shared, needs to be met. We need to live now rather than worry about the future. This will allow us to make the most of what we do with our time, what activities we take on, how we engage with our community, how we nurture our friendships.

- We need to adapt creatively and positively. We need to welcome the walking stick and the spectacles, and even the hearing aids, and discover how many opportunities and incentives there are to overcoming the barriers of ageing. My father-in-law was walking the Lakeland Fells well into his eighties, and our local folk dance group in Weardale has an impressively wide age range. While we have the gift of time, the gift of years, every moment is important and has potential. We are called to find our hidden creativity, and our hidden adaptability, and "bloom where we are planted". And we need to adopt the positive mantra of "Yes, we can", and to become "can do" people rather than "can't do" people, ready to accept whatever opportunities are on offer.

- We need to accept reality, and the mystery of what God has "wrought in us". We are unique, and we need to learn to know and love ourselves as the person whom God has made for this moment of time in this place. Reality may be challenging, but it is the "given" that we have to live with. I think of an older couple in our church, both now in wheelchairs, and with the most radiantly infectious smiles that light up any encounter. Perhaps it is the art of cultivating grateful self-awareness, blemishes and all.

- We need to believe that every phase of our life can be lived to God's glory, and that his purposes never fail. This is not always easy and we may reach stages when we wonder whether the road could not be a bit less rough and uncomfortable. We may encounter serious illness, chronic pain, restricting disability, and may find such faith and trust in God's purposes challenging. But ultimately we need to learn to accept that the changes and chances of this fleeting life are not random but are instead part of God's plan and will work to his glory.

- We need to have no regrets, but rather thanks, and to count our blessings. It is very tempting to look back in life, particularly as a reluctant solo traveller, and to say: "If only". In Psalm 42 the psalmist starts with a lengthy lament and backward look to happier times, but ends by saying: "O put your trust in God, for I will yet give him thanks, who is the help of my countenance, and my God."[26] We need to be at peace with God about the past if we are to be at peace with him about our future. And we need to be able to count our blessings, "name them one by one, and it will surprise [us] what the Lord has done".[27]

I spent much of my working life as a probate lawyer, both administering the estates of those who had died, and advising people on their Wills. It is an immense privilege to help people to consider the final stewardship of what they own of this world's goods, to consider how they wish to pass on to family and friends the benefits that they have enjoyed in this life, to consider ways in which they can leave their own individual legacy for the next generation. It is also a privilege to be alongside those who are bereaved, providing the support and advice to help them through the practical and legal complexities that can arise on death.

The people that I encountered were old and young and from all walks of life, because death, or the prospect of death, can be a relevant reality at any time, and in any place. If we are serious about our stewardship of what God has given to us then making a Will is important at any age. If we are asked to cope with the death of someone close to us, it may be our spouse, partner, parent, child, friend, and it may involve a network of other people, and this can cover a wide age range.

Dealing with death and dying in one's working life brings you face to face with the reality, but it does not necessarily make you comfortable with it. I remember visiting one undertaker to arrange a funeral and his young assistant admitting to me that, despite her job, she was afraid of death. If we are honest, we all probably share her feelings to some extent, but as Christians there is a hope set before us which allows us to view that "great unknown" with greater equanimity. The problem for those of us who travel solo is that we have lost our closest travelling companion with whom we could share these hopes and fears.

One of the things that I notice as I get older is that Christmas letters are moving from recalling all the travels and adventures of my friends to recounting their aches and pains, their latest operation or ailment. It can be a reality check, but while growing older is inevitable, perhaps growing up is optional. You are only as old as you feel, and there are as many spritely octogenarians as there are prematurely geriatric fifty year olds. Perhaps we need to accept more readily not just the limitations but also the opportunities that each age and stage brings. We can aim to grow old disgracefully, wearing purple and rejoicing in the eccentricities in Jenny Joseph's poem "When I am Old", while also accepting that old age is not for wimps.

There is a well-known prayer, reputedly written by a nun in the seventeenth century, that gives incomparable advice to those of us who are getting older. It is worth repeating here, with its hefty dose of realism:

Lord, thou knowest better than I know myself that I am growing older and will some day be old. Keep me from the fatal habit of thinking I must say something on every subject and on every occasion. Release me from craving to straighten out everybody's affairs. Make me thoughtful but not moody; helpful but not bossy. With my vast store of wisdom it seems a pity not to use it all, but thou knowest Lord, that I want a few friends at the end.

Keep my mind free from the recital of endless details; give me wings to get to the point. Seal my lips on my aches and pains. They are increasing and love of

*rehearsing them is becoming sweeter as the years go
by. I dare not ask for grace enough to enjoy the tales
of other's pains, but help me to endure them with
patience. I dare not ask for improved memory, but
for a growing humility and a lessening cocksureness
when my memory seems to clash with the memories
of others. Teach me the glorious lesson that
occasionally I may be mistaken.*

*Keep me reasonably sweet; I do not want to be a saint
– some of them are so hard to live with – but a sour
old person is one of the crowning works of the Devil.
Give me the ability to see good things in unexpected
places and talents in unexpected people. And give
me, O Lord, the grace to tell them so. Amen*

"Old" is of course a relative term, and I remember in my
twenties thinking that people I encountered in their thirties
and forties were really quite old. Likewise, death is no
respecter of age. Wherever we are on our solo journey,
and whatever our age, we must acknowledge that death
is a "given" that has to be recognised, that our mortality
is something to be befriended. Those of us who have been
bereaved have already faced this mystery of life and death,
but it is as we ourselves get older that this befriending of
our own mortality becomes more urgent and necessary.

Our Christian tradition sets before us a mystery of
faith and hope. A local friend is embarking on training to
become a Reader in the Church of England, and one of

her assignments was to ask members of the congregation to read the Nicene Creed – that long statement of faith put together by the early church only after much theological debate – and then to say, honestly, whether they really believed all of it, or whether there were elements of it that they found particularly difficult or puzzling. This initiated some interesting discussions over coffee after the Sunday service. Many people found it easier to endorse the concepts relating to a creator God and to the historical Jesus, than to endorse the statements about our eternal future. It is at that stage that we find ourselves restricted by earth-bound language used in describing concepts that are beyond our comprehension and imagining. What do we actually mean by "the resurrection of the dead"; by "the life of the world to come"; by Jesus "seated at the right hand of the Father"; by his coming in glory "to judge the living and the dead"? The apostle Paul found these things difficult to explain in his various letters to the early churches, and the church leaders who met at Nicaea had equal difficulties before they came up with the agreed statement that we now recite as a creed. Yet these doctrines relating to the future seem very real because we know that they affect us; they are the essence of the great unknown that we will all face when we come to the end of this life.

I love the concept of the communion of saints, and as I get older I become very conscious both of the saints whom I have known and loved who have already died, and also of the many people around me who radiate faith and hope in their eighties and nineties and assure me that life is always there to be lived to the full. They are indeed shining examples, and perhaps a humble ambition might be to learn from them. News that Ian's godmother had died gave me pause for thought – she had maintained contact with her godchildren, keeping in touch with me after Ian died, and she had reached the age of ninety-seven years having been a widow for thirty-two years. I realised that, like Ian, her husband too must have died in his mid-sixties, in his prime, at the point when they were retiring from overseas missionary work and looking forward to the next stage of life. And I realised that we do not know how many years we will have on our own, be it three years or thirty, so we need to be attuned to God and be willing to step out into whatever he offers. Then we can look back over that time of "travelling solo" with thanksgiving and without regrets, recognising another different and creative period of our lives. We may not welcome being on our own, we may not welcome the prospect of our own death, but God has given us the gift of years, and we need to welcome that gift and use it to the full, however many those years may be.

John Rutter has written a hauntingly beautiful arrangement of the poem "For the beauty of the earth". As it raises its "joyful hymn of praise" there is one verse which always resonates with me and even threatens to bring tears to my eyes:

For the joy of human love,
brother, sister, parent, child,
friends on earth and friends above,
for all gentle thoughts and mild;
Lord of all, to thee we raise
this our joyful hymn of praise.

I find myself thinking of the friends above, of those whom I loved and now miss, and as I get older this number increases. It brings a mingling of sorrow and gratitude, an acceptance of loss, a rejoicing in memories, and a valuing of the "friends on earth". Perhaps it gives me a brief insight into the mystery of the "communion of saints". In its celebration of the wonder of God's world, this poem gives a context for our mortality. All is gift. God gives – generously, and God takes away – in his wisdom. Perhaps Wesley's familiar hymn helps us to reconcile this outworking of God's mercy and love in our fallen world: "'Tis mystery all! the Immortal dies: who can explore his strange design?"[28]

Mortality is an elephant which we need to befriend and greet with confidence, and then we need to park it in a layby and get on with travelling on along the road ahead of us, enjoying our gift of years. Our travelling days are not yet done, and the road goes on, and on…

For the beauty of the earth,
for the glory of the skies,
for the love which from our birth
over and around us lies;
Lord of all, to thee we raise
this our hymn of grateful praise.

For the beauty of each hour
of the day and of the night,
hill and vale, and tree and flower,
sun and moon, and stars of light;
Lord of all, to thee we raise
this our hymn of grateful praise.

For the joy of human love,
brother, sister, parent, child,
friends on earth and friends above,
for all gentle thoughts and mild;
Lord of all, to thee we raise
this our hymn of grateful praise.

For the joy of ear and eye,
for the heart and mind's delight,
for the mystic harmony,
linking sense to sound and sight;
Lord of all, to thee we raise
this our hymn of grateful praise.[29]

12

Travelling On

"You are older than the world can be,
you are younger than the life in me..."

... What will the future hold for me?

The road goes on and on... the years stretch ahead and this is a continuing journey. How do I find the narrative that will keep me going? How do I rejoice in the past and have trust for the future? Where will I see God at work around me? How can I learn to say with confidence the words of Dag Hammarskjöld: "For all that has been, thanks. For all that is to come, yes".

* * *

Tempus fugit – the years roll by and the journey continues to unfold. Sometimes we can ignore the passage of time, and sometimes it compels our attention. Major anniversaries and celebrations can be the focus that forces us to stop and think, where we look back to the past and forward to the future. We mark centenaries of major events, we value silver, ruby, and golden wedding anniversaries, we take special notice of each decade of our lives. I found the experience of my seventieth birthday and entering my eighth decade to be one of those times both for real celebration and for profound reflection. My children encouraged the element of celebration with a party, a lovely gathering of lovely people, all of whom had been significant to me at different times over the last seventy years. Unbeknown to me each of them had been asked by my daughter, Liz, if they had photos of me that they could contribute for a slide show at the party. The resulting presentation was an amazing walk down memory lane, starting with the one-year old on a rug in the garden, and ending with the first-time author signing books at a book launch in Peterborough Cathedral. We laughed and reminisced and had champagne and balloons and cake. The element of profound reflection came later as I savoured the fun and the memories we shared, the very varied paths our lives had taken, and our hopes for the future.

As I thought about the party I contemplated the seventy people who had been invited, and the fifty who were able to make it and join us on the day. I had looked round the room and seen before me a brief review of my life. There were people from my childhood and my school days, from university, and that interlude that had been post-uni/pre-marriage; from the rich tapestry of our married life as Ian and I moved round parishes and jobs in south and north London, Durham, Sussex, and Peterborough; and now solo retirement in Durham and Weardale. These people were some of the family and friends who had populated my life. The family network was wide – it included three generations, with my three grandsons rising to the occasion and looking angelic and behaving impeccably; it included my two brothers with no illusions about their younger sister; it included my "in-law" family of Cundys, always so wonderfully supportive to me. The network of friends was equally wide, including a childhood friend whose mother had been at school with my mother in New Zealand, those with whom Ian and I had shared godchildren, my Palace "gang" who helped with episcopal entertaining in our Peterborough days, various former colleagues. Especially important was a group of four of us, who met over fifty years ago as giggly girls studying in London for university entrance exams (in the days before the more streamlined central UCAS system was created); we had remained a close knit "gang" of four through the eventful intervening years, and now we were embarking on a year of celebrations together for our seventieth birthdays. All of these were people with whom I had weathered the ups and downs of life, people with whom I had celebrated both life and death, people with whom there had been mutual support and encouragement, people with whom there were bonds of shared joys and shared sorrows. I was conscious also of the family and friends who were not present: those invited who could not come, those who were too ill to travel, and those who had died. And then there were the many, many other people – friends, acquaintances, colleagues, distant relatives – those encountered over the years and forming an important part of my life both past and present, many still a close and active part of my life, and some for whom contact had become more spasmodic. Revisiting our lives in this way can be an amazing experience, prompting thanks for the way that this rich cast of people scattered over so many places and times has contributed to the pattern of our lives, helping to focus on the things that have really mattered in the past, rejoicing in the present, and realising the potential that may still lie ahead.

More profound reflections also came as I looked back over my life's journey in another way. At the beginning of my seventieth birthday year I had done a course on spiritual direction, and one of our early tasks was to draw a timeline of our lives, marking on it the important events in our personal story, relating them to other things that were happening in our immediate context or in the world around us, and relating them to our perception of our spiritual growth. It proved to be a fascinating exercise, and surprisingly revealing and moving. I had also found that for me it was a disciplined exercise in charting all the ups and downs in my life, in tracing their relevance and context, identifying the major influences, and in noting the turning points. It was an exercise in seeking to discover what has made me the person who I am, to answer the "Who am I?" question, to reveal personal identity. It is an exercise designed to provoke profound answers if we were willing to seek them and expose them. And I found that looking back in this way was linked to people and places as well as being linked to events.

It was a valuable exercise as I realised how much the world had changed over those years, how much I had changed as I grew and matured, how much had been fitted into those years and the wide variety of things that I had done. It contained achievements and failures, random events, surprises and mysteries – all the ingredients of a good story. Yes, there were wrong decisions, dark days, times of hurt and hurting, but I realised that I could look back with acceptance of my story in its entirety. This is important because we are often tempted to go down the route of "if only…", when actually such regrets only serve to deflect us from being truly grateful for the good times, whilst acknowledging the reality of the bad times and our need for forgiveness. Acceptance is a great gift; it allows us to be at peace with ourselves, and allows us to look back and count our blessings.

The Anglican lectionary of daily Bible readings has been for me a useful discipline and it can be a gift to our spiritual lives, sometimes providing a very apt "word in season". On my seventieth birthday the readings for Morning Prayer included this verse from Paul's letter to the Corinthians:

"God is able to provide you with every blessing in abundance, so that you may always have enough of everything and may provide in abundance for every good work" (2 Corinthians 9:8).

Paul is writing in the context of arranging a contribution from the church in Corinth toward a gift to relieve the poverty and needs of the new Christian community in Jerusalem. So he is reminding the Corinthian Christians that they enjoy a comfortable lifestyle and are in a position to share their riches with others who are less fortunate; they should do so willingly and not grudgingly. And Paul's words are quite forthright: "He who sows sparingly will also reap sparingly, and he who sows bountifully will also reap bountifully… God loves a cheerful giver" (2 Corinthians. 9:6, 7).

As I read this "birthday" verse it seemed as though I had here a blueprint for the future, both a confirmation of blessing and an incentive, and I found that three things stood out for me:

(1) God's generosity in providing "blessing in abundance".
Paul has no doubts about the character of God, and about his ability, his will, his desire to bless, and Paul emphasizes the abundance of that blessing and of God's gifts to us. We find Paul repeating this emphasis on abundance and enabling power in a letter to the church at Ephesus when he refers to God "who by the power at work within us is able to do far more abundantly than all that we ask or think" (Ephesians 3:20).

(2) God's provision of "enough".
God's power may be limitless but in reality our needs may be finite, and so God gives us "enough". He is not in the business of encouraging profligacy, and it is not in his plan to allow us to wallow in unnecessary wealth and riches for our own sake. Why? Because…

(3) God's purpose is for "every good work".
God's gifts are given for the purposeful outcome that we may "provide in abundance for every good work". They are given to us in a context of onward giving, and we are called not to live to ourselves but to look outward.

So as I reflected on my life's journey so far it was a reminder to me of God's immense generosity to me. I have always been fortunate to have "enough", but at the same time I grew up in the post-war years of rationing, of "make do and mend", and with an ethos of sufficiency where extravagance was not encouraged. It was good training for the early days of marriage to a curate whose stipend in the late 1960s was £550 per annum – we learned to do "101 things" with mince, make our own clothes, and go on camping holidays. And God's generosity has continued in so many ways, both great and small. However much or little we may have, it comes as a challenge to those of us who feel that life has taken an unexpected and unwelcome turn that we need not only to count our blessings but to wonder how we can share that generosity.

Do I count my blessings sufficiently? Am I really thankful? The words of the General Thanksgiving come to mind again, it being one of the prayers that we had to learn by heart in my school-days (in the wonderfully poetic language of the Book of Common Prayer):

*Almighty God, Father of all mercies, we thine
unworthy servants do give thee most humble and
hearty thanks for all thy goodness and loving
kindness to us. We bless you for our creation,
preservation, and all the blessings of this life, but
above all for thine inestimable love in the redemption
of the world by our Lord Jesus Christ, for the means
of grace and the hope of glory.*

There is great beauty in these words, and an eloquent call to us to count our blessings, and to be thankful for whatever it has pleased God to give us. So we start with our life itself as an amazing gift, and then whatever health and wealth we may, or may not, have in addition is the context where God has put us and asked us to live that life. The mantra that Ian and I learned when we visited our link diocese in a deprived part of Kenya comes to mind again: "God is good, all the time. All the time, God is good". People who by our Western standards had very little of this world's goods taught us to praise God for his goodness in everything, great or small.

And the General Thanksgiving ends with the prayerful reminder that "from those to whom much is given, much will be required":

And we beseech thee, give us that due sense of all
thy mercies, that our hearts may be unfeignedly
thankful, and that we may show forth thy praise,
not only with our lips, but in our lives; by giving up
ourselves to thy service, and by walking before thee
in holiness and righteousness all our days.

Wow! That is some call to selfless service, and I continue to find it challenging. I am still blessed with the "enough" that God gives and I need to hear what God is calling me to do with my time and my talents, as well as with my money and possessions.

So as the road goes on and on, I find myself looking forward with anticipation and enthusiasm. There are still new journeys for me to make, both literally and metaphorically, and I am still blessed with health and strength and a restless spirit. I feel that I still have experiences that I want to share, that I can still be useful, that there is still a world to be cared for, that there are still people I want to encourage and accompany on their journey, and that the unexpected may still be around the corner. I still want to have the courage and the confidence to say "yes" to the range and variety of life's opportunities. Dag Hammarskjöld's words continue to inspire: "For all that has been, thanks. For all that is to come, yes." I want to feel free to push on new doors and see if God will open them and say "yes". I want to join with Kaylin Haught in her unconventional poem as she asks God mundane – even flippant – questions, and finds that "God Says Yes to Me", in unexpected ways...

> *I asked God if it was okay to be melodramatic*
> *and she said yes*
> *I asked her if it was okay to be short*
> *and she said it sure is*
> *I asked her if I could wear nail polish*
> *or not wear nail polish*
> *and she said honey*
> *she calls me that sometimes*
> *she said you can do just exactly*
> *what you want to*
> *Thanks God I said*

And is it even okay if I don't paragraph
my letters
Sweetcakes God said
who knows where she picked that up
what I am telling you is
Yes Yes Yes[30]

The future continues to unfold, and I am not alone on this journey, so may all of us who are travelling solo know the reality of God's "YES!"

*

Lord of life… travel with us on our journey
Lord of tomorrow… draw us into your future
Lord of time… hold us in your eternity.[31]

Notes

1. Line here, and at the beginning of each chapter, is taken from "One More Step Along the World I Go" (Sydney Carter 1915–2014) © 1971 Stainer & Bell Ltd. Used with permission.

2. Sydney Bertram Carter, "One More Step Along the World I Go", Stainer & Bell Ltd, 1971.

3. Adapted by my mother from George Cooper's "Only One Mother".

4. Tom Gordon, "Seasons of Grief", taken from *New Journeys Now Begin*, Wild Goose Publications, 2007, www.ionabooks.com. Used with permission.

5. From *A Common Prayer* by Michael Leunig, HarperCollins, 1990.

6. Shaker song by Elder Joseph Bracket, 1848.

7. Variant reading of Isaiah 49:15, 16, found on a prayer card.

8. From "The Weaver" by Grant Colfax Tullar (1869–1950).

9. "Blessing for the Traveller" can be found in *Benedictus*, John O'Donohue, published by published by Bantam.

10. Revelation 4:1, ESV.

11. Paul Torday, *Salmon Fishing in the Yemen*, Orion, 2007, pp. 222–23.

12. Extract from "Will you come and follow me?", words John L. Bell & Graham Maule, copyright © 1987 WGRG, c/o Iona Community, Glasgow, Scotland. www.wildgoose.scot. Reproduced by permission.

13. 1 Corinthians 10:13.

14. John Ernest Bode (1816–1874), "O Jesus I have promised".

15. John Clare (1793–1864), from "The Invitation".

16. Clive Evans, *Time Out of the Ordinary*, used with permission.

17. 1 Peter 3:15.

18. R. S. Thomas,"The Bright Field", can be found in R. S. Thomas, *Collected Poems 1945–1990*. It is a poem worth searching out and reading, but sadly permission to quote it is currently being refused on the unusual grounds of "over-use"!

19. The opening line of W. H. Davies' poem "Leisure" taken from *From Songs of Joy and Others*, 1911.

20. Variant found on a prayer card from St Mary's Abbey, West Malling.

21. "Behold, I make all things new", words John L. Bell, copyright © 1995 WGRG, c/o Iona Community, Glasgow, Scotland. www.wildgoose.scot. Reproduced by permission.

22. John Ernest Bode (1816–1874), "O Jesus I have promised".

23. Matthew 13:31, 32. Taken from the NIV.

24. Michael Sadgrove, *I will trust in you: A Companion to the Evening Psalms*, SPCK, 2009, p. 41

25. Michael Sadgrove, *I will trust in you*, SPCK, 2009, p. 45.

26. Biblical reference according to The Psalter in *Common Worship*.

27. Chorus of Johnson Oatman, Jr's (1856–1922) "Count Your Blessings"

28. Charles Wesley (1707–88), "And Can it Be?".

29. F. S. Pierpoint (1835–1917), "For the Beauty of the Earth", adapted in *Hymns Ancient and Modern, Revised*, 1950.

30. Kaylin Haught, "God Says Yes to Me", from *The Palm of Your Hand*, Tilbury House Publishers, 1995.

31. Copyright © Archbishop's Council

Acknowledgments

I am grateful to the many people whom I have met on my travels who have contributed to my journey into a new life as a solo traveller: to patient friends and family who have read and advised on various iterations of the text as it evolved; to church groups with whom I have tried out some of the themes I have explored; to clergy friends who have argued some of the finer points of theology with me.

Above all I am grateful to David Wilkinson, Principal of St John's College, Durham, who has continued to encourage and mentor me; to the late Susan Kent, Rector of Stanhope Benefice, for her insights and wisdom; to Caroline Welby, whose friendship and support I have enjoyed since Justin was an ordinand at Cranmer Hall, Durham, for writing a generous Foreword; and to Jenny Muscat, my editor at Monarch, for her patient and ever-helpful guidance in bringing this project to fruition.